Travels in China

Travels in China

ROLAND BARTHES

Edited, annotated and with a foreword by

ANNE HERSCHBERG PIERROT

Translated by ANDREW BROWN

polity

First published in French as *Carnets du voyage en Chine*
© Christian Bourgois éditeur / IMEC, 2009

This English edition © Polity Press, 2012

Polity Press
65 Bridge Street
Cambridge CB2 1UR, UK

Polity Press
350 Main Street
Malden, MA 02148, USA

ISBN-13: 978-0-7456-5080-7

A catalogue record for this book is available from the British
Library.

Typeset in 11.5 on 15 pt Fournier MT
by Servis Filmsetting Ltd, Stockport, Cheshire
Printed and bound in Great Britain by the MPG Books Group

Every effort has been made to trace all copyright holders, but
if any have been inadvertently overlooked the publisher will be
pleased to include any necessary credits in any subsequent reprint
or edition.

For further information on Polity, visit our website:
www.politybooks.com

— Contents —

— Foreword —

Roland Barthes left for China on a trip that lasted from 11 April to 4 May 1974, in the company of François Wahl (a philosopher and at the time an editor of books on the human sciences at Seuil, where he published, among others, Barthes himself), and a delegation of the *Tel Quel* group, composed of Philippe Sollers, Julia Kristeva, and Marcelin Pleynet. The official invitation extended to Philippe Sollers and the *Tel Quel* group, then going through a 'Maoist' phase, came from the Chinese embassy, on the initiative of Maria-Antonietta Macciocchi, the author of *Daily Life in Revolutionary China* (English translation 1972). The trip was to be an organized and supervised three-week tour, paid for by the participants. Though they would be welcomed by writers and academics, the travellers would actually follow a pre-established itinerary, visiting factories and tourist sites, attending shows, and going to restaurants – all part of the common experience of Westerners visiting China in the 1970s. The Chinese Luxingshe Agency provided the guides, the political spokespersons, and the material organization of the journey, and ensured that the visitors were protected from any contact with the Chinese outside the circuit defined in advance. Barthes regretted the absence of any unpredictable elements in all this, the lack of any 'fold' or 'incident' (that which 'falls' in the 'fabric of days').

The French arrived in China right in the middle of the campaign against Confucius and Lin Biao (the so-called 'Pi-Lin Pi-Kong campaign'), which led at every stage of the journey to ideological 'snapshots' of the political situation, conveyed by a ritualistic phraseology (what Barthes calls 'bricks'). Barthes's notebooks present a cool appraisal of this journey, attentive to details, colours, landscapes, bodies, and the little events of everyday life, which he comments on with humour. The notes he makes on things he sees, hears, and feels alternate with remarks inserted between square brackets: reflections, meditations, criticisms, or expressions of liking – so many 'asides' on the world around him. Certain words also recur, expressing his weariness with regard to stereotypes ('Etc.'), or a slight sense of distance ('Outside. . .').

Right from the start, Barthes had been thinking of bringing back a text from China. He filled three notebooks on this theme, in blue biro or felt-tip. The two first notebooks, 'Spiral Crown', with a blue hardback cover (Notebook 1), and a red one (Notebook 2), respectively, brought with him from France, are complemented, for the end of the journey, by a Chinese notebook, smaller, in black moleskin, bearing a quotation by Chairman Mao printed in red on the first page (the last, in the order used). These three notebooks are entirely paginated in red felt. Barthes reread them, set out a contents page for each of them, and drew up a thematic index in a fourth notebook.

On his return, Barthes used these notebooks to compose the presentation on China that he gave in May 1974 to his students in the seminar at the École Pratique de Hautes Études.[1] But he also prepared an article, entitled 'Alors, la Chine?' ('So, what about China?') (published in *Le Monde* on 24 May), which

---

[1] This seminar was published in 2010 as *Le Lexique de l'auteur. Séminaire à l'École Pratique des hautes études 1973–1974, suivi de Fragments inédits du Roland Barthes par Roland Barthes*, ed. and intro. by Anne Herschberg Pierrot, with a foreword by Éric Marty (Paris: Seuil, 2010).

attracted criticism.[2] There followed four articles by François Wahl ('La Chine sans utopie' ['China without utopia'], *Le Monde*, 15–19 June), then an entire issue of *Tel Quel* in autumn 1974 ('En Chine' ['In China'], no. 59), in which Philippe Sollers, Julia Kristeva, and Marcelin Pleynet (in an article continued in number 60) expressed in turn their opinions of China. Julia Kristeva reflected on her 1974 trip to China in her book on Chinese women (French edition *Des Chinoises* published 1974 [Paris: Éditions des Femmes, republished Paris: Pauvert, 2001]; English version *About Chinese Women*, translated by Anita Barrows [London: Boyars, 1977]), which contained photographs of the trip. Marcelin Pleynet then published fragments of his journey: *Le Voyage en Chine: Chroniques du voyage ordinaire 11 avril–3 mai 1974 – extraits* (Paris: Hachette, P.O.L, 1980).

A little over thirty years later, Barthes's notebooks, hitherto unpublished,[3] comprise an often very lucid view of the events and speeches of this trip. They show a phenomenological attentiveness towards the China of 1974, one that is more interested by people and things than by museums and archaeological sites. 'Reading through my notes to make an index, I realize that if I were to publish them as they are, it would be exactly a piece of Antonioni. But what else can I do?' (Notebook 3).

Anne Herschberg Pierrot

---

[2] The text was published separately by Christian Bourgois, a year later, with a hitherto unpublished afterword, reprinted in Barthes, *Oeuvres complètes* IV, pp. 516–20.

[3] A few pages from Notebook 1 were published in facsimile in the catalogue of the exhibition 'Roland Barthes' held at the Centre Pompidou, Paris (27 November 2002–10 March 2003), edited by Marianne Alphant and Nathalie Léger (Paris: Seuil/Centre Pompidou/IMEC, 2002), pp. 209–25.

Note on this edition

The reader will find below a list of abbreviations and acronyms used. Barthes's notes are indicated by asterisks, and the editor's notes are numbered. They are complemented by an index of proper names.

Most abbreviations have been spelled out in the interests of readability. Likewise, Greek is transliterated. Thanks are due for help with Chinese words and names to: Anne Cheng, Mlle Yan Liu, and Laurent Sagart. Thanks also, for their help with this volume, to: Nathalie Léger, Claude Martin, Alain Pierrot, Marcelin Pleynet, and, for his attentive reading and his advice, François Wahl.

Abbreviations and acronyms used

F. W.   François Wahl
Ph. S. Philippe Sollers
Pl.   Marcelin Pleynet

GPCR Great Proletarian Cultural Revolution
WPS   Workers Peasants Soldiers
CCP   Chinese Communist Party
PCI   Italian Communist Party

Works by Roland Barthes

OC I–V: *Oeuvres complètes*, new revised edition, corrected and with an introduction by Éric Marty (Paris: Seuil, 2002) (vols I–V).

Translator's note

Barthes often transcribed Chinese names into phonetic French: I have put all Chinese names into pinyin, with the exception of one or two that are now domesticated English names such as Chiang Kai-shek (in pinyin, Jiang Jieshi) and Confucius (in pinyin, Kong Fuzi). Barthes was fond of capitalizing words that one would expect to be in lower case: I have preserved his capitals, and generally respected the note form (occasional lack of punctuation, etc.) of his jottings, except where this would lead to unnecessary lack of clarity.

KAZAKHSTAN

UZBEKISTAN

TAJIKISTAN

KYRGYZSTAN

AFGHANISTAN

PAKISTAN

XINJIANG

GANSU

QINGHAI

Yellow River

Yangtzi

TIBET

Yangtzi

SICH

NEPAL

● Lhasa

BHUTAN

INDIA

BANGLADESH

YUNNAN

R U S

MONGO

THE REPUBLIC OF CHINA

▬▬▬▬ National frontiers

▬▬▬▬ Provincial borders

MYANMAR
(BURMA)

LAOS

THAILAND

RUSSIA

HEILONGJIANG

MONGOLIA

INNER MONGOLIA

JILIN

LIAONING

Yellow River

Beijing (Peking)

HEBEI

Tianjin

NINGXIA

SHANXI

SHANDONG

Yan'an

Xi'an

SHAANXI

Luoyang

HENAN

Yellow River

JIANGSU

ANHUI

Nanjing

Shanghai

EAST CHINA SEA

HUBEI

Wuhan

Yangzi

Hangzhou

Chengdu

Lushan

ZHEJIANG

Yangzi

Changsha

HUNAN

JIANGXI

FUJIAN

Taipei

GUIZHOU

GUANGXI

GUANGDONG

Guangzhou

Shenzhen

Xiamen

TAIWAN

HONG KONG

PACIFIC OCEAN

VIETNAM

HAINAN

NORTH KOREA

SOUTH KOREA

JAPAN

NOTEBOOK 1

— Notebook 1 —

11 April 1974

11 April. Departure, washed from head to toe. Forgot to wash my ears.

Aeroplane: in other words: hanging around, being immobile, not travelling.

Echo in *Le Quotidien de Paris*. They're expecting a *Return from China* and *Afterthoughts on China*.[1] But what if they really got: *Afterthoughts on My Return to France?*

Orly. Delayed. Ph. S buys a *saucisson* and some bread in the duty-free and we have a bite to eat in the lounge. Dinner on the plane. Empirical experience ought to imply that, since we are squeezed in, cramped by countless prosthetic devices, we get served with very simple things; but, of course, empirical experience is countermanded by the French vice (title of a play by Labiche): window dressing:[2] *moules* with a salad, veal in gravy, greyish, greasy rice – two grains of which fall, inevitably, onto my new pair of trousers.

As I furtively kissed his hand in a public place, he said: you're scared someone might see us? And I replied: no, I'm not scared someone might see us; I'm scared somebody might see how *old-fashioned* this gesture is, and you might be embarrassed.

Take-off from Orly: in a separate mass, a dozen Chinese in black jackets with standing collars, though the guide is in a business suit. They look like a travelling monastery.

12 April

On closer inspection (on the bus to the runway), the seminarians have jackets of a very different blue: regimental uniformity from a distance, individual differences from close-up – the 'officer' collars are really small.

A whole plane full of Europeans (Italians, Germans, French) for Beijing. How disappointing! You always think you're the only one able to go there.

Go back over the echo in the *Quotidien de Paris*, show the lousy ethics it's based on.

How boring! To have the downsides of fame (the echo of a private trip) and none of the (financial) advantages.

If I were to be executed, I'd ask people not to bank on my courage. I'd like to be able to get slightly drunk beforehand (on Champagne and food).

They're huddled at the back of the plane, their eyes closed, like – might I say this affectionately? – little pigs, plump little animals; they're penned in too, in a sense.

I'd like to say, to J. L., to R., cynically (but they'd understand): become, in writing, *someone*.

In theory, China has a thousand possible meanings: historical, ethical, etc.; our great discoursers can talk about them after their own fashion (L. S.,[3] Granet, etc.). But for the French, China has only one meaning, set out in a highly credible way in their papers. But this plural is itself on *our side*. A leap of the intellect: from the plural to one.

Four hundred visa applications have just been rejected.*[4] The hostess is surprised we're travelling; she says: 'Are you *in the know?*'

Arrival in Beijing

'So, what about China? . . .'
Young soldiers: the impression of nothing under their tunics. Smiles.
Airport lounge: plain, austere. Leather chairs. Switzerland fifty years ago.
A big red rectangle.** Support Surface.[5]
Road from the airport, straight, with willows on either side.
We go past a dog, a young European out jogging in shorts.
The interpreter: the weather is 'nippy'.
Fetish object: the big thermos of hot water for tea, embellished with flowery transfers, which girls, and boys, hold.

Saturday, 14 April[6]
(Beijing)

Overcast sky. Slept badly, pillow too high and hard. Migraine.
Yesterday evening: meeting with the guides. Small lounge in the hotel. Big armchairs, crocheted shoulder rests.
'Politeness' and cameras.
Austerity: linen not ironed.

Glance through the window at six a.m. Badminton. One of them plays very well, they have a knock-around – just a few moves, the way you smoke a cigarette.

---

* Because of Jean Yanne's film. (*The notes indicated by an asterisk are by Roland Barthes unless specified otherwise.*)
** Two green shrubs in front of it.

Their bodies? Wizened and elastic. A bit bag-like.

No sexual difference.

All of a sudden, one of them, a vague erotic electricity: the reason is his intelligent eyes. Intelligence equals sex.

But wherever do they put their sexuality?

I feel that I won't be able to shed light on them in the least – just shed light on us by means of them. So, what needs to be written isn't *So, what about China?*, but *So, what about France?*

Processions of schoolchildren with Red Flags. Brecht.

Try and find the *Colour*. Blue greys. Red splashes. Iron. Khaki. Green.

Tiananmen Square: Groups. Walking in step. Whistles.

Choir. Stereophony.

Marseillaise.

Schoolteachers, male and female.

Bag, flask. Kids. Crypto military.

Twelve–fourteen years old. They hold hands. Girls: bag, short jacket + short trousers (Bicycle Clips)*.

Meanwhile sun, breeze. All quite charming . . .

Give and take in the regimentation. There are some left apart.

The old folks are even more marvellous than the young.

No attractive skin.

Sateen, velvet.

Fine hands. Eyes that squint. Pockmarked faces.

The 'Chinese Schoolmarm' type.

Big butts. Clowning around.

---

* and also the way they splay their arms and fingers a bit.

Glossy beige of the tiles in the Forbidden City.
What will remain of Beijing? A breeze, a haze, a mildness, a light blue sky, a few snowflakes.

Haircuts are coded.
What an impression! The complete absence of fashion. Clothing degree zero. No elegance, or choice.
Flirtation is foreclosed.
Another fetish-object: the (electrified) loudspeaker held by a woman schoolteacher.

Garden. Japanese plum trees, blossoming magnolias. Rockery.
Little girls at play, dancing around a double rope – varying their steps – instead of leaping up mechanically.
Little picnics for the children in groups. Bread roll, choc-ice, apple.
Desert of Flirtation.

Effect of transformation produced by the total uniformity of clothes.

This produces: silence, lightness, not vulgarity – at the price of an abolition of eroticism.
A kind of Zen effect.

Two young boys put their arms round each other's necks. But at a later age – after fourteen – none of them do this. So repression. So sexuality?
The very few good-looking ones are curious, stare at you – beginnings of a flirtation?

11:35 a.m. First sign of sexuality. A bold chap in khaki and his mate stare at Julia with sly grins.

Smells. Cabbages on the Square. Palace Museum. Wet dog, cheesy manure, sour milk.

2 p.m. Lugou Qiao.
People's commune of Sino-Romanian Friendship, or Marco Polo Bridge Commune.[7]

Li Sian. Commune and Revolutionary Committee Vice-President.[8] Mme Ho Shiu Young. Head of the Commune administrative bureau.
– Merging of five cooperatives.
– Performing services for the city.
– Vegetables: last year, 230 million pounds + apples, pears, grape, rice, maize, wheat; 22,000 pigs + ducks.
[Long table covered with light-green waxed cloth. People on both sides. Clean. At the far end, five huge painted thermoses (their samovar)]
Stages: Mutual aid group → Cooperatives → People's commune[9] = increased production → following certain principles: 1) Mao: the Commune is good. 2) 'Get organized'. [He[10] knows his dates and his figures by heart]
[On the wall: Mao + quotations + a painted plan of the commune. Chairs along the wall]
Tea is served: in pot-sized cups again.
Why these results?
– levelled the fields
– irrigation works. 550 electric pumps
– mechanization: tractors + 140 monoculture workers.

[The tea girl, pink face, peasant type, placid, white teeth and plaits, stays to listen]

Transports: 110 lorries, 770 carriages.

= 11,000 families = 47,000 persons.

[The guide talks to us as if we were close acquaintances]

= 21 production brigades, 146 production teams.

= 10 workshop-factories (repairs, machines for ploughing. Bricks).

All this well-being has been accumulated by us ourselves. Everyone who works receives over 600 yuans per year.[11] Our own efforts, no need to request state investment.

Mao: 'We need to focus on the health problem in the country-side.' Free medical care (apart from registration). Fifty barefoot doctors.[12] Every team has one or two doctors, every brigade a care centre. Commune: a clinic.

[We are served from the thermos again]

Education: 50 secondary schools + 19 primary.

Every year: 20 candidates for University, elected by the Commune.

80 shops: all articles the same price as in the cities.

Clothes: partly provided by the Commune.

Many deficiencies remain. Level of mechanization.

Visits

Shops. We are applauded. Fruit (apples, grapes, pears. Strong smell).

Big thermos in wickerwork.

Very clean and tidy.

A house (the weather is very fine). Real little squares of vegetables.

The Mother's discourse:

Before the Liberation, etc.[13]

1949 the Chinese Communist Party liberated us from ruin.

1954 we took part in the primary cooperative.

1955 we built these five rooms.

Three boys, four girls. The oldest boy at the factory (24 years old).

Electricity.

Her husband: Brick factory.

[I reflect: all the women in trousers. No more skirts*]

Surplus money: to the Savings Bank.

'Life now really excellent. Comparison with the past: heaven and earth.'

[This whole visit to a house: like the visit to the Dutch house on Marken Island]

Now, Women have the right to study, go to the cinema, etc.

Daily schedule: 5 a.m. wake up.

6 a.m. Fields. 7:30 a.m. Breakfast.

Break at 10 a.m.

12 noon Lunch.

1:30 p.m. Work → 3:30 p.m.

Then Rest, etc. → 7 p.m.

Evening: sometimes cinema.

Work: every day: receives work points (28 days for the men, 26 for the women). No Sunday. Rotation.

Every ten days, half a day for politics + three times a week, study. Today: critique of Confucius and Lin Biao. Lin Biao: wanted to return to the rites to keep the peasants in poverty. We stigmatize him.[14] [This is the woman, speaking with authority]. Confucius wanted to restore slavery, Lin Biao too, he copied Confucius.

* The traditional costume was with trousers.

A few pots of geraniums.

In the street, with its sides built of mud.
On the wall, a Blackboard. A poem in chalk.

Second house. Fenced-off garden, little fruit trees blossoming. The daughter is twenty (the one who served us tea at the beginning): sometimes she too writes poems (and reads heroic novels).

A moment of fulfilment, of assent, of agreement: two classes, one on English, one on physics (on Force).
They applaud. Faces. School things are poor and clean. A sense of charity. And after all, they applaud us so nicely!
Chemistry class. In every place a basin and a tap.

Ping-pong. Ph. S plays. Through the big glazed windows, the fine clear daylight and young trees.

Electricity. Charming teacher in a blue outfit.*
All of this is erotic, at last.

These classes. At the back of the room, are there bad guys, shady characters, people with the wrong ideas?
'NEEDS HELP'.

Clinic. Hydrochloric acid. Puddles on the floor. Five barefoot doctors including a charming woman, Japanese, who shows us round the clinic (she is wearing an over-long white coat – as if she were in disguise).

---

* His hand, soft and warm – and I discover that he's a worker.

Evening. Puppet show.

Big suburban hall. Heavy smell of disinfectant (cf. the Clinic).

A crashing bore, and inescapable: we end up penned in with two rows of elderly European females. Impossible to mingle. The organizers don't want us to. Hands off bodies. Exclusions.

Night: the worst migraine of my life – insomnia and nausea. Distress, worse, panic. This, I am starting to think, symbolic of a wholehearted rejection of the day, the stark contrast between: Yes nothing to say and, no I don't want to (the fetishist's *Yes but*).*

Reminder: Perhaps all political discourse acts like an object of psychic investment, of release, which also enables them to be non-antagonistic, smooth. Let's make a sacrifice to a big piece of Doxa and all the rest of the Discourse (bodily, instinctual) is free.

Sunday, 14 April
(Beijing)

Overcast sky. Cold wind.

Printing works (Xinhua)[15]

Handwritten posters with caricatures. Confucius and absurdity. Caricature of Confucius's skull, he's hideous. Next to it, a balloon with a very pretty mother and baby (Lin Biao said that his father and his mother had given him a handsome face).

Another image: Lin Biao's plane crashes.[16] [So the stereotype gives rise to 'inventions'].

---

* Vomiting out the Stereotype, the Doxa.

— 14 —

Endlessly repeated Doxa: Lin Biao and Confucius had the same point of view.

The Factory Official + worker from the printing works. Very nice blue lounge. Sky-blue armchairs all round the room. We sit in them as if they were stalls. Oriental perfume. Four Marxists on the wall (including Stalin).[17]
The Official welcomes us.
1949. Initially 100 workers. 6,000 square metres. Grew to: 3,480 persons, 8 Workshops.
[The official had offered us cigarettes, in round green boxes. Tea]
[Always this very tightly constructed, very clear, initial speech: very bracing, facts and figures]
Prints of Portraits and Magazines (North Part of the Factory). South: Marxist books and reviews – an illustrated one called *China*, 17 different languages – + Albanian Review[18] + minority national reviews + *The Red Flag* review + Novels (*Red Flag*, 2 M. 200,000, North China) – 10,000 tonnes of paper.
The Official attacks the Liu Xiaoqi line: they were against portraits, and published feudal books. With all of this, the old factory was paving the way, via public opinion, for the restoration of Capitalism. Luckily, along came the Proletarian Cultural Revolution.[19] [Here, insertion of the brick:[20] fight victoriously against the influences of the Liu Xiaoqi clique, etc.]
[Ah if only I could carefully record these bricks and show their combinatorial rules]
Now: Mao's *Selected Works* 40 million, *Red Flag* 100 million.
+ Marx Mao study movement in the broad masses of our factory's workers: 80 study groups outside working hours.
Against Lin Biao. Rectification of the style of work. All the personnel are launched on the Campaign. During the socialist

transition, the political line comes first and foremost. They are in the middle of liquidating the crimes of the Lin Biao clique. [This guy: the greatest density of bricks. How many per yard of phrases?] A real sermon-speech. Another brick: 'Over 2,000 years ago, Confucius wanted to return to the rites. Returning to the rites meant restoring the lost paradise of the dynasty. . . .'
[So, the greater the culture* (of this Printer), the denser the stereotypes become ≠ the West]
Lin Biao wanted to restore a hierarchy that flourished in the feudal period. Confucius wanted a politeness that did not apply to the people. Confucius and Lin Biao were just the same, *ejusdem farinae*. [Endless repetition of the parallel]. We are at the start of this campaign.
Still things which leave something to be desired.

It's not disinfectant any more, it's petrol.

Lin Biao, a scapegoat who can be made to fit every occasion, every couple of minutes.
Over a corridor, a black and red slogan. Welcome to the *Tel Quel* group.
[Obviously, in this factory with its high intellectual level. Posters on the *Critique of the Gotha Programme*,[21] etc.]
More merits in the Cultural Revolution? – more than in the People's Commune.

Huge piles, in the corridors, of hagiographic images.
Sometimes a delightful smile, heart-melting (a little worker perched on his big rotary press churning out images for Albania).

---

* Admittedly a purely political culture.

Ph. is very interested in the posters, which are many and copious, and this lengthens the visit. Personally, I prefer the rotary presses and the bodies (men and women) operating them.
The most desirable of them are among the workers.
Young women workers in blue outfits and little white caps.
This is the Xinhua Printing Works (New China).

[Moments of extreme interest and extreme distress]

[It's always the same: the proles are good-looking – heart-melting, needing help – but as soon as they become Cadres, their faces change (our guides, the Official). It's insoluble]

Blackboard. The advantages of the Cultural Revolution. Little items (bicycle, radio, clothes, pigs) with the fall in prices. [This Printing Works is very Cultural Revolution.] But this also seen through an anti-Lin Biao bias – he said everything was better before.

Classification of characters. Girls in three-sided compartments. The characters are classified by frequency (the most heavily used first).
Room for casting the type. A table with four little girls, classifying characters. They are school pupils: one month of manual labour. It doesn't look very unpleasant – not very hard work.

Everywhere banners saying 'Welcome to *Tel Quel*'.
If only we could see French factories like this! *Tel Quel* in France?
Every workshop: applause. '*Tel Quel* and its friends are applauded in the factories of China'.

tel quel
comme ça

'But is it really rightfully yours, M. Barthes, this applause addressed to you by workers?'

Posters all in calligraphy, glossy chalk colours.

The only important point, always, everywhere, is the daily and universal reconstitution of bureaucracy (of hierarchy, of division).

Very important: abolition of Manual/Intellectual, i.e. of Hierarchy, of Bureaucracy.

Final (verbose) speech given by a very vivacious little guy.* Lin Biao wanted to separate Mao from Marxism because it was not Chinese. The workers reacted: they can very easily understand Marx-Lenin (Lin Biao said not, but said that Mao *was* easy: for example the *dazibao* on the *Gotha Programme*). Lassalle seen as the same as Lin Biao (reactionary plot).[22]
Mao: class struggle continues every day in a socialist period. Lin Biao said, on the contrary, that the Cultural Revolution had liquidated the reactionaries all at once.

* Head of the communist league, the Young Communists.

[Rarely a reply to a concrete question ('who are still the class enemies in the factory?'). There are: facts and figures, and bricks]

Dazibao = collages made by workers to teach the cadres to know what the problems are, to have confidence in the masses.[23]

'The Great Proletarian Cultural Revolution'.

[They seem to be afraid of personal relations with each other. You don't see them. I was quite astonished to see in the street outside the factory a worker greeting the Official.]

Lunch at the airport.

Zhao, the guide: Have you read Hegel?[24] – No, if it's not necessary for political Practice. People read what can be related to practice.

Trenchant, a bit mechanistic, a hint of national complacency, our guide calls out for teasing by endlessly having neurotic problems presented to him.[25]

(Reminded of the visit to the printing works and the speeches that were made there.) The Doxa is very powerful, made up by cementing together blocks of stereotypes; but since combinatorial rules are involved, one can still read, and even decipher, the words (living, meaningful) via the *omissions* or the *marks* of certain stereotypes.

In addition: living, individual thought ('political awareness', analytical aptitude) must be read *in the* gaps in the fabric of stereotypes (whereas for us, to make something new, escape from endoxal mortification, it's the stereotypes themselves that need to be killed).

Beijing–Shanghai plane (1:15 p.m.)

Brand new Boeing. Several caps in fake American style. The hostesses: the khaki outfits, the hair in plaits or bunches, no smiles: the opposite of western simpering.

No smiles, not on any occasion.

Our baby hostesses, austere and plaited, serve us with a plate, a knife, a pear (of the sweet turnip kind) and a warm towel.

Typology of feminine hair styles:

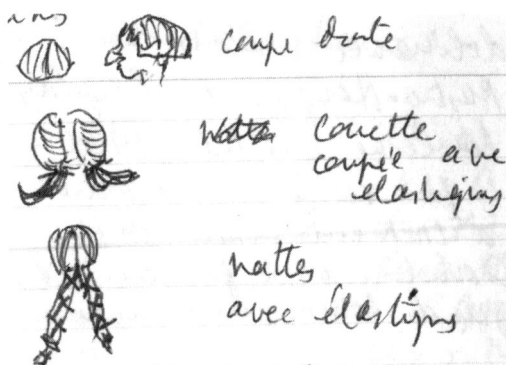

2:55 p.m. Shanghai. 14 degrees: grey and not warm, a few drops of rain.

Warmer. Palm trees. Mimosas. Perfumes.

Welcomed by three in navy blue, one of them a writer at the Shanghai Publishing House. Are they more intellectual? Less touristy. Glasses (variations, a typology?).

A lot of people, more attractive.

Several signs in pinyin[26] (both are taught, apparently).

(Peace) Hotel: euphoria, deliverance. Vast, calm. Austro-Hungarian and English. Marlene Dietrich 1930.[27] The port opposite. English district with huge buildings.

Hotel room with two windows. Cupboard as big as a room.

Small meeting with welcoming party in a little lounge overlooking the port, brown sail, little sail hoisted high up. Table with white napkin, armchairs, cigarettes, tea. Presentation by Comrade Ye Ya Li, writer, editor. Protocols: speech, etc.

Quick walk round the hotel. Intense curiosity; everyone follows us, stares at us. Intense gazes.
A lot of friendly couples.

A walk round the hotel by myself. Alone at last. It does me good. Saw a few clothes shops.
Dinner at 6 p.m.

Evening: Big Shop No. 1. Stationer's. Jackets. Crowds of people.
Then the Friendship Shop. Fake Antiques. Paintbrushes, pictures mounted under glass.

Monday, 15 April
Shanghai

Grey, quite cold.
Breakfast. Over a terrace opposite, the port, sails in the background, there's a guy taking his time doing his solitary gymnastics: no muscles, no bones either – what? 'Loosening up' his body? Dao?[28]

Yesterday, pleased at finding the word in English, 'speech'. But, and it's better, Zhao says: 'chat'.

Towards the Naval Dockyard. We go through an extensive working-class district. Coalmen on tricycles, smoke wafting off lumps of coal. Stop in the car before taking the ferry. There's a boy playing with a catapult, three women of the three different ages washing clothes in a wooden tub, with a plank like in Morocco, a lot of people go by, a lot of tricycles, baskets, movables, pigs sliced in half, big brooms, thick ropes and cables.

(Yesterday, in the car, this recommendation again: don't photograph the *da₂ibao*, they're part of Chinese domestic affairs.)

Revivifying crossing of the Huangpu. Smell of Fish. Big wooden raft. Immense brown goffered sail.

A wan sun.

Three rough boys. One sings. Music on the raft. The small boat with goffered sail. What colours! faded, a hint of yellow, faded rust, beige, nougat . . .

On the other side of the river, it's the countryside. Yellow patches of rape. Women – real mannish types, green wicker hats, working on the canal system.

Naval dockyard. A feast of *da₂ibao*!

A big banner, carefully written: Welcome to *Tel Quel*.

Toilets. 'Ladies'/'Gentlemen'.

Lounge, tea, cigarettes. A woman welcomes us* (Revolutionary Committee. There are three young people, two women** + one very small guy with piercing eyes).

Comrade Can (from the Committee) tells us about the dockyard (ocean-going freight and river boats. Construction

---

* Administrative cadre.
** Trade union, Working-Class Women.

and Repair). 7,000 workers including 1,400 women. 10 workshops.

Before Liberation: refitting[29] of the boats overseen by bureaucrats. Only 700 workers. Reduced repairs. Today: 100-tonne cranes. After Liberation, Dockyard returned to Chinese People. Major development. Great Proletarian Cultural Revolution. 1969: high seas shipping, 10,000 tonnes [link between the Cultural Revolution and Productivity]. [Myth of the construction of the High Seas Ship: Great Exploit, Prestige. The ship *Wind and Thunder*, beginning of a poem by Mao.]

[Shanghai tea is much less nice than Beijing tea, which was golden and perfumed.]

Workers: against the revisionist line of Liu Xiaoqi, who said: It is better to rent or buy than to build.[30]

[All these revolutionary announcer-presenter officials: edgy little people, full of life, smiling.]

For High Seas Ship of 10,000 tonnes, the hold had to be overhauled (cf. *infra* visit).[31] Already 6 ships. Now, another hold being built for ships of 20,000 tonnes.

[The official is the one with a good grasp of the figures. He can speak well, and structures his 'speech', delivers it clearly, without embellishments but with the appropriate political bricks. He is a Rhetorician.]

Visit of the Ship *Fenguang* (161 m × 20.4 m).

Shipping capacity: 13,000 tonnes.

[Crafty little eyes looking here and there, full of laughter, a tuft of hair high on the forehead. As small as a child, an edgy, charming doll.]

Dockyard-Visit.

More wicker hats.

Cale
(= rampe)   Me,

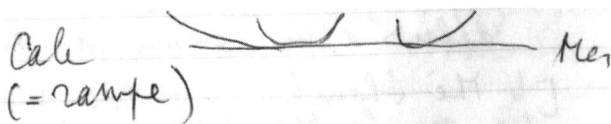

Very young welder. White outfit. Little round dark glasses.
Pink neck over the outfit. Blue ribbon on the green wicker hat.

Civilization without phallus? High birthrate? You just need a
small, potentially tumescent conduit.*

There are boys constructing a big wooden awning for *daẓibao*.
We visit a huge workshop of machines presided over, as if they
were church organs, by solitary young workers.
I notice that our little official has white, manicured hands.
They make us wear wicker hats and white gloves.

Visit of the Ship. The Captain's Cabin. Photo of Mao on a plat-
form, with a cigarette holder in his hand.
(The ship, undergoing repairs, does Shanghai–Japan.)
This makes me dream.
Yet more fine calligraphy by Mao (Poems) on the wall. Gold
on red.
From the poop, a splendid view over the bow and the wake in
the river; big boat in the middle. Clear sky.
Young worker, perfect oval, purity of his eyes, of his eyebrows.

In the lounges too, *daẓibao* on blackboards (by a fifty-four-
year-old mechanic, who says he is happy to be travelling on a
Chinese boat, thanks the Saviour Mao for giving him a revolutionary conscience.) Oriental perfumes.

* Written on seeing a very ugly but sexy young worker. It's so rare . . .

[Sexuality: the mystery remains – and will remain – intact.]

[The writer – he always wears a cap, apparently because of his baldness: it's clamped on. He puts his helmet on top]

Workers: everywhere, it appears, they work in a calm, relaxed, attentive manner, with frequent breaks.

Discussion (back in the small lounge). [Liu Xiaoqi and Lin Biao are evaluated with respect to the dockyard. The first: rent rather than buy, buy rather than build. The second: wanted to build very large tonnages to rival the advanced dockyards in the rest of the world: this is the ultra-leftist right-wing line – cf. the quotation, in the ship's dining room, by Mao, on being prudent rather than rash.][32]
It's the woman who provides the answers: very concrete.
Set theme (expressed by the woman): could 10,000 tonne ships be built on a hold of 3,000? The technicians said no; but the revolutionary mass of workers, consulted [theme of political practice] said yes, etc. Set theme of the Nanjing Bridge ('The revolutionary line of Chairman Mao').[33]

Girl (the third): Role of the unions: organize the study of Mao's principles: organize the working masses as the main force in the current critique. Promote production. Competition in the workshop. Train new administrative cadres among the workers, receive the opinion of the masses on the management of the naval dockyard. Sports, artistic activities (Basketball, Ping-pong, Cinema, Theatre sketches for the workers).

In the car, on the way back from the naval dockyard (it is midday, a bit overcast, rather oppressive, I'm sleepy, on the verge of a migraine). Ph. S uses the words 'voluntarism' and 'pessimism' in connection with Lin Biao (I don't remember in what context), Zhao the guide lays into me: a muddled speech, in which the passionate, not unexpected message is the set theme on Lin Biao, that hypocrite, who tried to sabotage the achievements of the Cultural Revolution, etc.

Something bizarre and wonderful (after a while) – that emaciated writer in his cap, who reminds me of Foucault, smiling and completely silent, who accompanies us everywhere as a writer (in other words as a *talker*).

[So, their discourse: a combinatorial system of bricks, in which the very small degree of free play allows differences to emerge – doubtless requiring subtlety to decode. For this is not our code: this linguistics is not Saussurean. No idiolect. They probably have no discourse for love, for sociological information, etc.]

Afternoon of 15 April
Fine weather

Visit of a new residential district. San Qua Lung. Liberation Alley.

A sort of private Housing Development. In one room: tea, cigarettes, table. Presentation (woman from the Revolutionary Committee – of what? – of the district). Workers' residential area [as we arrive: the inhabitants have all lined up and applaud us].

Greets French friends and *Tel Quel*. 35 buildings, 1,800 homes, 7,000 men. Workers + teachers, doctors, employees. All the public services. Primary school. Crèche. Food. Workshop for spare parts. Hairdresser's, bookshop, bank.

Before: impoverished past. 1937, Japanese militarist aggressors. Districts bombed.[34] 1941, a lot of refugees begging. Oppression of the property owners: district crammed with poor. Sharks are the same the world over. For even a hovel (see the photo on the wall) you had to pay the local despots.

[Deadly 'speech', comparison between past/present. Draw up a list of set themes.

I look at my glass of tea: the green leaves have opened wide and form a thick layer at the bottom of the glass. But the tea is very light, tasteless, barely a herbal tea, it's just hot water.]

After 1963, four-storey houses. 1967, 16 July: everyone moves in. Party time. Inhabitants bought portraits of Chairman Mao. They were moved to tears. The poor have no definite destiny. Freed thanks to the Party, to Chairman Mao. [Sentimental discourse: *di yin*.[35]]

Two hundred retired workers: retirement granted them by the Party and Mao. Retirement in body, but no ideological retirement: we still need to give our services for the sake of socialist edification; we need to be volunteers.

[Uniform clothes? Of course. And yet, what differences, however subtle! Grey or black jackets: functionaries, cadres, etc. Blue jackets, workers, etc.]

The old people help with the children's education. Relate memories of the old society. Edifying episode: a child finding 40 fens in the street and giving them to the revolutionary committee. Why? The children replied: so as to observe the principles of Chairman Mao, etc.

Retired workers: another task: cleaning up.

Rent. Per month: 30 fens, 1 m².

Visit (more applause): Workshop: Women: electric relays* eight hours a day. Ten tables, five machines per table + other work. It's a little shed in the residential district. Outside, it's a nice day, trees, old people, children. It smells like an English sweet. In spite of the sun, it's glum: eight hours a day? The women are ugly. They don't speak.

Zhao, in the sunshine (I've popped outside): 'In the past, women: housewives, at home, objects. Now (nods at the workshop), they are liberated; not for money, for emancipation, building socialism.'

Second workshop (electricity again): women only, apart from *one* boy; sickly. 'He has a chronic illness, but he can work.'

Museography! a little island of hovels from olden times, a sign above the entrance. Charming alleys! A peaceful little flower garden.

An old man (72 years old) shows us three kennels: his former dwelling (he was a rickshaw puller for twenty-seven years). Set theme of Gratitude. Set theme Past/Present. [Here: Theme of the Poor.]

* Batteries?

[The writer, still here: I notice that his trousers have turn-ups, and are well pleated.]

The old man (set theme, continued): illiterate. After the Liberation, he managed to take evening classes, he can read. Admiration for Chairman and Party.

Fit of the giggles! The old man: In 1972, an Italian called Antonioni . . . Antonioni . . . Antonioni . . . But the Italian people friendship for the Chinese people. Antonioni two-faced: didn't want to film the five-storey building, filmed the museum-hovels (reserved for education of children's class); Antonioni rolled on ground to film! Insulting the Chinese people.

Antonioni: same words as Soviet revisionism, Lin Biao and Confucius sang the same song.[36]

All of this: the old man in front of the kennel. [What a fit of the giggles!]

Crèche. Children three and a half. Little red ballets. Little girls with make-up, red lips, red cheekbones. Red ribbons on the tops of their heads.

Perform a sketch: the small coin picked up in the street handed over to the policeman.

Harmonium accompaniment. Their movements: very Madame Butterfly.

Another room. Another ballet. Raised finger.

Third room. Small boy: Hello. Sketch. We are going to perform military acts. Always the little finger, the fingers separated. Half in disguise.

Visit to an apartment. A retired woman worker.

Four generations, eight people. Three rooms.

Thanks to Chairman Mao we have the right to welcome foreign and French friends.

In society before, etc. . . . the women had no rights, etc.

Set theme of Society Before. [Distinguish between the Set Theme and the 'Speech'.]

She develops the Set Theme, with personal incidents (one day she dozed off, the foreman hit her, etc.).

[The Story, the Repetition, the lesson: the *lectio*.]³⁷

[Rising anti-stereotype nausea.] I'm too tired to take notes on the set theme, which is very long.

'Life' (story), in the hagiographic sense.

Retirement: Woman: 50 years. Man: 60 years. 'We aren't lagging along ideologically. We need to respond to the benevolence of Chairman Mao, we need to give our services, helping with the children's education.'

Provisional end of the Set Theme. Questions. Arrival of the Great Proletarian Cultural Revolution Set Theme. With this, something more interesting: mention of differences within the family, the woman went through a phase when she was again attached to conservative groups. She was gradually awoken by her son.

Outside, standing up, a girl is knitting with four needles. A young lad is eating a bowl of rice with herbs; he hits a smaller boy, who starts to cry and runs away.

So, the session is in two parts: 1) the set theme, the Story, the *lectio*; 2) thanks to the questions, the idiolect to some extent reappears, the emergence of 'character' (ah, no, the cliché immediately returns: Lin Biao made her realize that she needed to oppose the restoration of capitalism).

In the district, weekly meeting (Thursdays) for the local

residents to criticize Lin Biao, Confucius. Pull out the weeds by the root.

Now it's the Return to the Rites that makes an appearance.

The Set Theme is a language. It does not exclude sincerity, life, etc.

Second house (that of Antonioni's old man). Nicely decorated kitchen with two old women cooking. It smells good. There are two toilets side by side: odd!

5:30 p.m. Discussion at the hotel.

1) Sollers: the Chinese demand for love.

2) Me: The only point: language. Otherwise agree.

Evening

Circus. 12,000 seats.

It's the Beijing circus that I saw in Paris with some gigolo, I don't remember which.

You don't know anything, I'll never know anything: who is the boy next to me? What does he do all day? What does his bedroom look like? What does he think? What's his sex life like? etc. Small collar, white and clean, slender hands, long fingernails.

Great success of a sound effects engineer. Do the Chinese like imitation? Criticism? The start of something?

Pi-Lin Pi-Kong campaign (*Pi* = to criticize, *Pan*: Down with)

批 林 批 孔

Dinner:

1) They have to be taken *literally*. They are not interpretable.

2) Body nearby (Circus). Presence – even in absence.

Tuesday, 16 April
(Shanghai)

Nice day, a bit chilly. Spring morning.

Hospital no. 2. Delightful gardens. Then, disinfectant.

Big lounge, Portraits. Big table with a *white cloth*.* Introduction.

Wan: Revolutionary Committee (he is a paediatrician) + Anaesthesia + Ophthalmology + Services,[38] Administrative Office.

Hospital, 1958, Leap Forward. Staff: 1,100 – 744 beds. Medical school, 3? pupils – 3,000 appointments a day.

Mao principles: 1) first prophylaxis. 2) Service provided to the Peasants, Soldiers, Workers. 3) Mass movement in the hospital. 4) European medicine + Chinese medicine.

1) Prophylaxis, Common and epidemic illnesses. Peripatetic teams.

[The tea is better: more golden, with jasmine.]

2) Europe + China. 30% of operations under acupuncture.

3) Scientific research: especially into common illnesses. Examples: chronic bronchitis in the elderly, coronary arthrosis, cancer, cataracts.

4) Education (University level).

There are still shortcomings.

Gastrectomy under acupuncture.

Very slow lift. Disinfectant. Everyone in white coats. We are disguised. Patient: 52 years. Gastric ulcer. Six needles: two, feet; two, abdomen; two, back.

---

* White tablecloth for speaking, not for eating. It's very euphoric.

A tall guy, good-looking, in blue, slowly dabs him with fluid. Near the head, an apparatus for electric stimulation. Half an hour for anaesthesia. Field of operation, rail in front of the patient's face.

The man in blue has no gloves.

The patient: eyes open, rather anxious.

(600,000 operations under acupuncture.)

Patient with arms stretched out. More successful on upper part of the body.

The surgeon: tall guy with glasses. Anaesthetic effect incomplete, sometimes. Section, incision. The patient's eyes are closed. Acupuncture. Criteria. Patients:

– not too fat

– no operation before

– mustn't be afraid (psychologically prepared, surgeon's explanations beforehand). Trial injections. Before the operation, a small dose of sedative.

The operation continues. Deeper incision.

Near the head, two nurses handle the needles for the head.

The stomach appears.

In a corner on a radiator, an old kettle, a bulldog clip on a piece of crumpled paper.

He opens and closes his eyes. The stomach gradually emerges. [Shrill noise of the translations while the patient is on the table.]

(Three-hour operation.)

He opens his eyes, tenses up a bit: he's feeling sick (the nurse pats him on the cheek). They give him a little water in his mouth so as to reposition the tube (to stop wind).

= Worker in packing. Party member.

There are thirty-five surgeons in the hospital.

Very often eyes closed. Pale.

10:20. Is the stomach out? His hand is not clenched. We leave the loggia in a group, in our disguises; at the bottom of the stairs the nurses turn back to go up. The patient seems to be staring at us, bewildered (no, there mustn't be any adjectives).

Then: we go through the Ophthalmology department; people in the corridors. Applause.

Film: cataract operation under acupuncture (Teaching of Chairman Mao). Very elegant demonstration.

Finally out of all that. Back to the peaceful Lounge, the white tablecloth, teapot-cups of hot tea, cigarettes, the sunny garden outside.

Conversation with the doctors:

Psychological causes of illnesses? Yes, but since we are in a socialist regime, very few mental illnesses able to trigger ulcers, etc. . . .

[Reduction to professional tensions: the car driver.]

Mental illnesses; external (social) causes: not common (caused by financial ruin, 'disappointment in love'(!)). They are cured by materialist Dialectic.

Shanghai: a psychiatric hospital = Mental illnesses with internal causes, nervous system, hereditary illnesses (schizophrenia, in part). They are against Freud, because of his sexualism, reality is not sexual.

Sexual tensions among the young? Focused on effort, study, work. Healthy life. Late marriage? 25 years for a girl, 28–30 for a boy: voluntarily accepted, not compulsory.

Sexual freedom before marriage? Considered as debasing; it's not accepted by young people.

Since the Cultural Revolution, new Acupuncture School: stronger and shorter stimuli ≠ Tradition: gentler, longer needles that stay in. But the same theory of Meridians. New theory: the stimulus is concentrated so as to attack the enemy (the main body of forces is concentrated, the stimuli); fewer points ≠ old school: 360 points, new school: 100.

This morning's patient: new method.

Acupuncture: appraised by the people for 2,000 years. No particular Philosophy.

Relationships between doctors and staff: Division of labour, but political equality. Relationships of camaraderie between doctors and staff. Important dealings: everyone. But no authority of doctors over staff.

[On all the Maos in all the lounges, the wart on his chin.]

Afternoon
Lovely weather

At the top of a seventeen-storey tower block (Shanghai Hotel). Terrace. Panoramic view (really beautiful). The whole of Shanghai, like Chicago. Brown city – and the car horns down there, constantly sounding.

House of the CCP (2:30 p.m.)

Looking at the photos presented.

1 July 1921. First Congress. Twelve Delegates including Mao. Time underground. House in the old French concession.

[Lounge, red-brown wood. Big portrait of the young Mao, thick black hair. Table with coffee cups.]

[Welcome, but we remain standing.]

Congress: four days here.

[Pulley suspension.]

Then sabotaged by a Chinese spy. Delegates forced to go somewhere else (a boat on a lake).

House occupied by an ordinary Chinese family. Room rented by a delegate.

All the furnishings, the crockery: reproduced, re-created.

[So what I thought were a lounge and cups for us were Museum mock-ups.]

In the next part of the same house: real lounge for presentations. Portrait, old Mao (with the wart). Tea. Very pretty cups (pale blue with white arborescences), cigarettes.

Official in charge of the Restored House: Historical speech.

[The tea is without leaves, insipid.]

Around 1920, 70 people, six groups in China + two student groups, France and Japan.

Mao the Hunan delegate.

[And always Marx, Engels, Lenin, Stalin in big coarse prints.]

List one by one of the twelve Delegates – and their deaths.

Four had joined for sordid lucrative reasons, renegades of the Party: their stories. (Liu Renjing: became a Trotskyist 1927. 1929, creates Left opposition organization to Leninism. Trotskyists in China: in guise of the left, undermined the CPP, in collusion with the Kuomintang.[39] He returned under a false name to Peking University, at the Liberation. Protected by Liu Xiaoqi. Cultural Revolution: denounced. Latest news told us that he was dead.)

Last delegate: Li Da, delegate from Shanghai. After Liberation, Rector University Wuhan. Dead in 1966, illness.

+ Delegates by Lenin (3rd International): a Dutchman Maring, Niknosky, Russian.[40]

All intellectuals (even the 70 members of the Party).

The Congress itself: its themes. [It's a real Lecture, well structured.*] Debate: either found a proletarian Party or found a

---

* And without any notes!

bourgeois reformist Party. Leftist line wrong: small group cut off from the masses, activities just among the small number of Chinese workers: wrong, because cut off from the peasantry. Rightist line, wrong too: opportunists: the Party is supposed to be limited to the mere propagation of Marxist-Leninist ideas without organizing revolutionary struggle; opposed to strict Party discipline; Party = Club.

Mao criticized these two wrong tendencies. Eventually, three decisions: 1) adoption of the first Statutes of the CCP; 2) define the Party's main task: develop the working-class movement, mobilize the working masses (application: 1921–3: Workers' Movement in full swing in China. 300,000 workers organized. But Mao also organized the Peasants, 80% of the total population); 3) election of the CCP leadership; general secretary: one absentee, the head of the Guangzhou Bureau of Education: Chen Duxiu.[41]

In 1927, crisis: 70,000 members reduced to 10,000 (Coup d'État by Chiang Kai-shek).

7 August meeting (Huan). Mao is present: power grows out of the barrel of a gun, etc., etc.[42] Expulsion of Chen Duxiu. All the rightist opportunists worshipped Confucius. Need to link Lin Biao and Confucius.

Chen Duxiu: veered towards Trotskyism. Ultra right = Ultra left! Chinese Trotskyists liaising with International Organization of Trotskyists. Chen Duxiu brandished the banner of the left but he wanted to liquidate the Revolution: on the left in appearance, on the right in essence.

The end!

The Ten great struggles of the CCP:

1. Chen Duxiu (Cf. *supra*).
2. 1927–8   Qu Qiubai, left.[43]

3. 1930   Li Lisan, left.
4. 1930–1   Luo Chang, right.
5. 1931–4   Wang Ming, left.
6. 1935   Zhang Guotao, right (during the Long March), defeatist line.[44]

Liberation

7. 1953–5   Gao Gang, right.[45]
8. 1959   Peng Dehuai, right.
9.   Liu Xiaoqi.
10.   Lin Biao.

[Huge room, austere, very clean. Bay window, red brown, looking onto small courtyard, sun – long table with glass top (lace doilies underneath). Set back from table, two rows of chairs. There is the Custodian of the Museum (the Speaker), the four interpreters, the Writer and a woman.] Mao alone on a wall stares at the four others on the other wall. Always the same.

Discussion (after a break): (5 p.m.).
Relationships with the 3rd International? Relationships with Trotskyism? (Rightism and Leftism.)
(The comrade doesn't want to be the only one to reply. Let everyone join in the discussion. He'll speak of his own knowledge.)
[We want to go to the cinema; but I'm sure that we won't be able to; it's always being postponed. Today we're told: in Nanjing. Probably because of the actual films. Not good enough?]
Reminder, from Mao, that they will never forget what they owe to Lenin, Stalin.
The mistakes of the left? Because those in charge weren't able to unite the eternal truth of Marxism-Leninism to the concrete practice of the Chinese Revolution.

[The woman, behind, taking notes, hands a note to the Speaker-Official. Who is she?]

Before 1927, 3rd International: role of guide. Then Stalin's erroneous opinions on the Chinese Revolution. But mistakes to be mainly laid at the door of the three Officials responsible and not to Stalin or the 3rd International, since they applied a dogmatic line, transporting what was Soviet to China, mechanically (didn't realize that Workers in China = a minority ≠ Peasants: great majority).[46] Another mistake: City ≠ Country (well-known theme).

[The demonstration: accurate, well known, slow, slow. The great *correctness* of the knowledge.]

'In spite of the mistakes made by Stalin at the end of his life (ideological level), Stalin remains a great Marxist-Leninist since he was always in favour of the Revolution.' If Stalin had died later, he would have managed to find a solution to the Soviet problem of class struggle.

Trotsky against the triumph of socialism in a single country. Ultra-leftist; claimed that the proletarian Revolution in Russia could be consolidated only by the outbreak of Revolution in other countries. And then, he opposed the union of workers and peasants. Stalin's struggle against Trotsky: justified. So, Stalin is not rightism and Trotsky 'leftism'; this is a falsification: deceiving the masses. Even in Lenin's day, Trotsky: anti-Leninist fraction. Lenin denounced Trotsky. Trotsky's deceptive remarks. Trotsky degenerated into a counter-revolutionary element (attacks on Soviet leaders); 1926, linked to English Espionage; rightly expelled in 1929. 1933: 4th International in Mexico. 1934: alliance with the Japanese. 1935, links with Hitler's Germany.[47] Counter-revolutionary activities, links with imperialism. No use brandishing his left-wing banner, helped imperialism to sabotage the Revolution: right = left.

Trotskyists in China: always few in number. 300–400 – then a few dozen. Kuomintang used Trotskyists to mislead revolutionary youth: very useful in sabotage. In fact, so-called leftists = rightists.

The end! 6:30 pm!

Visit to a bookshop.

Big tower block.

First storey: Luxun display.[48] New books advertised. It's big, rather empty. Visitors. No crowds.

Table with benches. People reading books, deeply absorbed, old and very young. Social-realist images.

[It's chilly. A cold?]

Evening after dinner. A group tour, just us. Full of people. What a good place for cruising! Buy things from the Friendship Shop.

Discussion.

Wednesday, 17 April
Shanghai

Nice weather.

Quick summary: an apparatus of undeniable effectiveness (as far as needs are concerned); the puzzle is unsolved on the level of values (of desires); here they are still only means.

Permanent industrial exhibition. Galliera.[49]

Hall: military-industrial style, uplifting. Bust, flags, cordons of light bulbs, illuminated red letters. Cheap Stalinist print.

Long-winded speech of the ? in the Hall. Welcome. Figures.

We look out over a hall of very clean machines, working away for nothing. At the far end, Mao standing, in plaster and in his coat, surrounded by red flags.

Oral presentation of a turbo-reactor by a slip of a girl with plaits.

[And always at the far end, the four mug-shot posters of the Germano-Russians[50] – facing Mao on the other wall.]

Machine for making screws. A young boy, for us, sets it going; he stares intently at us – his nails are well cared for.

Punching machine for biro clips.

Zhao – do you know about machines? – No, but I'm learning. – Good, you learn every day.

Visit: etc.: machines, explanations, young women. A European group, very ugly, follows on our heels. This endless series of pile-ups really annoys the director, who pushes and beckons us forward, with the rounded clear-cut gestures of a sacristan showing people around his church.

All I hear, at every machine, is: before the Great Cultural Revolution.

The director, a chit of a man who looks like Francis Blanche . . .

Model ships.

Hall of cars, lorries, tractors.

'Shanghai' make of car (our taxis) cf. Volga.[51] 130 km/h, 12 l./100 km. Magnificent reception car, open-topped. Its middle seat, propped up high, is convertible into a rear seat, at the press of a button. I have my photo taken in it with Julia.

We move on to textiles (lovely sunshine in the courtyards. It's 10:15 a.m.). The director has managed to separate the groups, forcing us to skip the textile display and then leading us back to it after the (awful) group of Bavarians.

Break in a kind of cafeteria. Wicker chairs. Tea. Cigarettes. Draughty. A fountain of flowers in the middle.

'Speech', after all that, by Francis Blanche.

[Green tea, insipid and luke-warm.]

During the speech on the machines Before/After the GPCR (Great Proletarian Cultural Revolution), I have in front of me on the wall a blow-up of horizontal calligraphy by Mao: utterly elegant (grassy calligraphy),[52] cursive, impatient, and spacious. Reflection on the 'frame'; my paintings: also calligraphic blocks; it's not a scene cut out, it's a block moving forward.

Around two tea tables, a small lively seminar; very soon they are discussing among themselves (on political questions).

It emerges that they have been humiliated again and again by the Soviets, who kept telling them things like: you won't be able to make anything more than toy cars, etc. But armed with Mao Zedong thought . . . (Great Leap Forward).[53] GPCR: the workers' initiative completely mobilized.

[All the same this country which, next to the cheap portrait-posters, shows an abundance of Mao's calligraphy: age-old elegance, poetry, personal form. It's an absolute counter-vulgarity.]

Rooms: arts and crafts.

Block of jade (Hunan): three tonnes. Sculpted. The red flag at the top: in agate. 12 craftsmen. 2½ years: mountaineers climbing the Himalayas. [But what is the jade which fascinated China? Silicon.]

Artificial flowers.

Knick-knacks in modelled rice flour.

(All of this hideous, as you would expect.)

Wooden sculptures: dishes, groups.

Under a magnifying glass, poem by Mao, forty-five characters on tiny block of crystal.

Medicine. Acupuncture needles.

Others, linked to electricity.

Model: a squashed rat with acupuncture needles.

The ear has almost all the acupuncture points for the whole body.

Traditional medicinal plants (in a jar) and products made from these plants.

Big model: atoms. Structure of insulin (1965).

Thermos. Sewing machines. Cutlery. Clockwork. Biscuits, jams. Photography. Musical instruments. Typewriter. 2,100 characters classified by their radicals. Sport. Ping-pong.

Another room (11:45 a.m.). Cinema. Short film: Acrobatic displays, pentatonic music.

Equipment for Radio, cinema.

Medical equipment. The guides hurry us along – to the great disappointment of the little woman demonstrator (there is one in each room).

Fabrics room.

Grand piano. Harps. Accordions. A young boy plays the grand piano very well; full of energy. Great technique. Tends to Pop!

Sculpted objects. Group. Mao in robe, workers, soldiers, peasants. It's just like the Sermon on the Mount.

Calligraphy by Mao. A lot of it. They're more and more beautiful. Their only work of art.

12 noon. End of the visit.

Return by car. (Bright sunshine, mild weather, spring): the crowd lines the streets throughout the journey. They are waiting for four hundred Japanese (a Ship), received by the Town Council.

Afternoon

[Just as, since we've got to meet some philosophy teachers tomorrow, we've been asked to prepare and submit our questions in advance, we've also got to have a conversation with the writer and our guides this evening, so this morning they've presented us with a list of questions about intellectuals in France, reviews, relationships with the Communist Party, the importance of Confucius in France, etc.]

Lunch. Depressing discussion among ourselves on the intellectual situation in France. Don't agree.

On the boat
(on the Huangpu)

Standing on the boat, under the sunshine. Very comfortable. Two charming waiters in white. Nice faces, not a trace of ill-will.

Behind, a charming veranda, wicker armchairs, table, cigarettes, red flag.

In the forward lounge: the Captain's speech (but another group turns up. It's spoiled!).

We leave. The captain returns. Speech. From here to Song (the Confluence of the Yangzi): 28 kilometres.

Boats, all sorts of boats.

And now the naval dockyard where we were yesterday (on the right).

Very beautiful: the big boats, at anchor, halted in the middle of the river, sometimes two by two, for kilometre after kilometre. And always sampans, sails with Brechtian colours.

After an hour and a half (at 3 p.m.) we reach the confluence with the Yangzi (after 28 kilometres, practically, of port, and boats of every kind). It widens out until the continuous line of a real Ocean: blue grey, boat in the distance placed against this immensity. Very impressionistic. We turn round.

An admirable junk: yellow, turquoise blue cabin, red traces on the keel. A certain fluting on the hull.

Smiles of the young tea waiter in white (those ones get really close. At other times . . .).

After four days – have a strong desire for a nice cup of coffee.

Latticed, padded sails.

I wrote to P. B. this morning, and this afternoon I miss him physically . . .

Last night a painful dream with the following theme: I'm in the midst of my guests, and there are many of them, but I'm excluded; I have a lot of friends but I don't have a friend. I fly into a temper, which increases my exclusion.

Back at the hotel at 5 p.m. Weather still fine.
Rest and postcards.
(No news from Paris and France since our departure.)

Evening 7 p.m.
Discussion

in a small lounge on our floor, in the hotel, with our interpreters and the Writer.
Longwinded speech by the Luxingshe boss[54] (a podgy little man with glasses).
Writer's introduction. 'Let's have a cosy, comfortable chat, about this and that.'
Our replies (Sollers):
1) a) French reviews of 'philosophy'?
— *Temps modernes*, Sartre (not at all well known)
— *Critique*, eclectic (*Piping ≠ Pipan*: to stigmatize)
— *Nouvelle Critique*. Quite a wide circulation. Has increased its influence (*La Pensée*). For us, theoretical struggle mainly against this review.[55]
— Weeklies. *Le Monde*. Union of the Left.
— *La Quinzaine*: anti-Chinese.
[They are very welcoming, cordial, attentive, talk a great deal among themselves]
Back to *Temps modernes*: more details.
b) Main subjects discussed:
a. Language.
b. Institutions. Power (Prisons. Right to shelter, Women,

Family, Bourgeois Morality, Youth). Crisis of Power. Education.

c. Human sciences. Psychoanalysis, Sociology, Anthropology.

d. Controversies within Marxism.

2) Object of Research in the field of philosophical theory?

90% of it in thrall to bourgeois idealism. Humanist empiricism. Technocratism. Scientism.

Althusser. His two periods.[56] And his pupils – have they left the CP?

3) Influence of the USSR and Revisionism on philosophical theory?

Direct USSR influence: very weak.

Influence of CP: very important.

CP: two heads 1) political: pro-USSR. 2) a façade to lure people in: generalized eclecticism, liquidation of Marxism-Leninism = dogmatico-revisionism (eclecticism).

[Ph. S.: is his massive, endless critique of revisionism sufficiently dialectical?] [Perhaps the Chinese critique of revisionism is more supple and dialectical.]

[It's funny, this oval table with its white cloth, with us around it and these Chinese of very different types, bespectacled, with their caps, their uniform smocks, writing at Ph. S.'s dictation.]

[This is Ph. S.'s big piece: his images flow, his elocution is self-assured, he looks at me, etc.]

Ph. S.: Contract proposed by the CP to petty bourgeois intellectuals: we will maintain order in the masses (the infra-structure), we give you the superstructure.

[Ph. S. completely scotomizes the leftist rivalry. All of it quite egocentric: all the press is viewed on the basis of the way it rejects *Tel Quel*.]

[Example, Pleynet presents the Ponge incident as evidence for fascism![57]]

4) Controversy between Marxism-Leninism and revisionism. Muddled controversy.

5) *Tel Quel*'s work.
No claim to be founding a political party.

6) Seuil.[58] Petty bourgeois. Very high degree of liberalism. Possible enclave.

7) Lin Biao Confucius in France? Up until now, confusion in France, incomprehensible. One of our tasks when we get back: make him better known and explain him.

[What did you do on this trip? – We worked!]

Last remarks by the Chinese. Luxingshe boss: We don't have any time left to tell you about our publishing. Pi-Lin Pi-Kong: we understand that you didn't understand everything. Nor did we: a movement that is starting to dig deeper; we who are taking part, we study (*Gotha. Imperialism Highest Stage* + Mao: *Correct handling*); mass studies – Marx, Lenin, on Feuerbach, Engels, this: good;[59] with the present time. Publication of brochures on Pi-Lin Pi-Kong. Shanghai Review: for example, article on the genius of Lin Biao and the innate order of the Heaven of Confucius, etc. Other articles.[60]
[The return of the *Gotha Programme* is interesting. Why this obviously concerted return – in the Pi-Lin Pi-Kong campaign – of Marxism's only utopian text?]
[At the prompting of the Writer – it was his evening, but he's

yet to say a word – we are given the number of the Shanghai Review.]
Discussion: Shall we continue? Yes, in anticipation of tomorrow.

The Writer's remarks on Confucianism and the Materialist Schools (first question for tomorrow) and the problem of the Doctrine of the Mean and Ultra Rightism.
Doctrine of the Mean: more or less reconciliation, eclecticism. Attitude adopted towards social contradictions: for example Lin Biao said that in our anti Soviet-revisionist struggle, we didn't need to go overboard, we didn't need to exaggerate; advocated reconciliation to cover Soviet Revisionism [this is what I've just written about Ph. S!] [said that just before the Cultural Revolution], and capitulate before it. So Doctrine of the Mean = in reality right-wing Opportunism: point of view of realist practice ≠ Doctrine of the Mean = metaphysics: in class struggle, a good-natured attitude! [I feel under attack.] Confucius: Doctrine of the Mean, since he wanted a return to the problem of slavery. Lin Biao: if the two sides wish to be reconciled, then they can become friends [all this coming from manuscripts in Lin Biao's residence]. Another example: Lin Biao: let's not carry on the struggle against Soviet Revisionism, otherwise we'll lose a friend. Lin Biao: a two-faced character; many of the things he was brooding on inside he kept to himself: he a process of revealing himself, we of uncovering him. Plan 571[61] requested the USSR's nuclear umbrella. With time, you French will manage to grasp the essence of this problem, like us Chinese.
Lin Biao's line: not at all leftist, but ultra-right. Managed to pass his line off as leftist.

Example: 'Restrain oneself and return to the rites'* = return to Capitalism. Same, attack on Mao: project 5, 7, 1. Chinese homophones: 5 = Army; 1, 7 = uprising, insurrection = armed uprising.

[Unfortunately the Writer is the most stereotypical.]

[All this is supposed to rest on Lin Biao's 'manuscripts'. – A posteriori.]

End of the session 10:50 p.m!

Thursday, *18 April*
(Shanghai)

Weather still fine, like in summer – but a bit muggy.

On the floor above a swarm of young waiters in white; they're doing sweet f.a., watch TV, have a natter, etc. It's really like Bangkok.

Suitcase.

A quick walk by myself. The quayside promenade is teeming with people (at every time of day); the port is magnificent, huge, Dutch, a cargo ship sets off, sails, etc.

Hazy sunshine.

[The nicest, gentlest of our three Shanghai interpreters: Jiang Jon King. Luxingshe.]

Session with the Philosophy Teachers from Shanghai

9 a.m. Little lounge in the hotel. Answers to the questions left by us yesterday. Five young people including one woman. Futan University.

1. Political sciences: Qu Tian Yang
2. Jing ?: Philosophy
3. Mrs ?: Philosophy

---

* Banner, four times in Lin Biao's manuscripts. Quotation from Confucius.

4. Fan Cuzi: History

5. Ying Bui Qan: Chinese language

1) Controversy over Confucius. Two antagonistic schools: Legalist/Confucianist.[62] A well-known set theme of the historian makes its appearance with regard to the question: Confucius: slave system ≠ Legalist: Rising property owners.

[Our jackets are brought. I'm glad to slip away. Trying on. Return. They're talking about land.]

[When they've been asked questions in advance, they come back with a lecture.]

[When the delegation comes in, at the beginning, i.e. the disclosure, the *'first time'* of bodies – isn't this rather like the entrance of partners in Sade? I fancy this one, not that one, etc.]

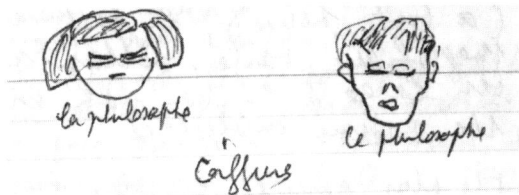

la philosophe

Coiffures

le philosophe

Very precise lecture, very historically detailed. A lecture in Marxist history.

[Trying to take notes, this morning, but I give up]

[We're in a 'suite' in the hotel, a room, two lounges, view over the port; at other times, a paradise to live here – the quayside down there for cruising . . .]

10:07 a.m. This history lecture on the Legalists is still going on.

[Analyse the Tea system in depth: long session, tablecloth, glasses in wickerwork covers, big Thermos. From time to time they pour more warm water into every glass. It's insipid. But, this, existing on the table, then in gestures, a protocol, a *spectacle*, turns the spoken word into something *indirect*.]

[This narrative is, so to speak, diagrammatic: it seems emblematic, by its characters, its situations, its forces, its struggles and even its episodes, to the (supposed) current Crisis.

Technique of the Chinese portrait

Superior, transcendent figure: the struggle for the restoration of the past.]

2) Our question: Lin Biao, and the parallel with Confucius? Residues of Confucianism in today's way of life?
[This morning the nice guide said to me: All ask the same questions, that way you'll eventually understand.]
It's the boyish (and quite sexy) woman philosopher who replies (see drawing on previous page).
Lin Biao: essentially right-wing, apparently right-wing.
[We've ordered a coffee. Great boldness and a great pleasure.]
Freedoms: Free market. Profits. Work norms in the production teams (≠ not today).
Sale of land. Loans with interest. Management of private enterprises.
All of this asked by Liu Xiaoqi and repeated by Lin Biao.
Was working to restore capitalism.
– But Lin Biao fought Liu Xiaoqi?
– He was hiding behind an attractive façade. He was continuing the Liu Xiaoqi line. In the 571,[63] he said he wanted to re-establish all the enemies (the landowners, the wealthy peasants, the bourgeois right-wingers), emancipate them on the political level. And on the international level: revisionist imperialism.
Lin Biao and 'Restrain oneself and Return to the Rites', the 'Doctrine of the Mean'.
These precepts from Confucius: actually political principles to return to slavery.

Doctrine of the Mean: supreme moral value of the slave-owning system. Confucius was opposed to social progress. Refused to draw a distinction between the main contradiction and the secondary contradiction. Now the solution of a contradiction: only through struggle, to engender another contradiction (Marxist teaching). Lin Biao: metaphysical attitude.

– Vestiges of Confucianism? – Revolutionary doctrine: vestiges in different areas of social life: for example, among intellectuals: contempt for the working class and peasant masses [didn't understand the question: ethno-sociological non-perception], idea of promotion by means of study, refusal of integration of intellectuals into the masses. Another precept from Confucius: one should behave in such a way that the people act without understanding. *Id.* Lin Biao: let the people think of oil, tea, soya, vinegar, salt, i.e. household tasks.

Five nblematic ubstances The Pi-Lin Pi-Kong campaign: raise the political level of the people. Lin Biao wanted to found a fascist dynasty of the Lin family.

[Often, it starts with set themes very far removed from the answer and then little by little it becomes more precise.]

Lin Biao: family of landowners and tradespeople. Capitalist Bourgeois.

– Role of Zhou Enlai in the campaign?

– Central Committee with Mao at its head. Unified leadership.

[A *Rhetoric* of these sessions needs be drawn up, going over all these notes: Plan of the longwinded speeches, Stereotypes (Bricks), Comparisons, Diagrams, Figures, etc.]

– Confucianism and Women? [The Woman replies – a very moonlike, gentle, well-scrubbed face.] Confucius: gives more importance to men than to women. Vestige among the people: contempt for Woman, belief that she is incompetent. Today: Women are emancipated on every level, their status considerably higher. Women all equal to men, politics and education. Full confidence of the Party in the teacher who is speaking.

– Will the critical work on Confucius be practised on the other philosophical schools in China?

– That is necessary, but at present, critique focused on Confucius since he long dominated feudal society. Other schools? The Legalist school? progressive in its time, but also reactionary, so needs to be subjected to criticism. *Id.* for Daoism, although less strong than Confucianism. All these schools of the past need to be critiqued.

– Among the ancient schools, any precursors of materialism?

– Marxist philosophy: completely different from past philosophies. In any case, assimilate them from a critical point of view, is useful.

Wang Tsun (Han).[64]

Wang Han Tseu. Certain dialectical elements. Argued against the theory of divine will.

– Is there anything positive in Daoism? – Representatives: from the masters' class: Dao (preceding the Heaven and the Earth) = Absolute Spirit, of Hegel, objective idealism. But struggle between Confucianists and Daoism: struggles within the masters' class. It was not the struggle between idealism and materialism.

3) Questions on education.

Philosophy? Linguistics?

– Philosophy courses: Classical dialectical materialism. Précis of History and Chinese Philosophy, and of History of philosophy in Europe. Critique of contemporary bourgeois*⁶⁵ schools. Political economy. History of the Labour Movement. Logic. Modern Languages.

Logic? – Its History is not taught. Formal logic (its formulae) is taught.

Linguistics? – Courses on Chinese language. Ancient, contemporary language, rules for writing: 'writing properly'?

– Yes. Criteria for writing properly? – Previously, teaching of mother tongue, but this was separated from the masses; Cultural Revolution: reform: mother tongue taught in relation to social research carried out by students → results of research drawn up. The students involved in participating in the reform of writing system: now simplifying characters – learning pinyin.

Differences between the way intellectuals and masses speak. So Mao recommended that intellectuals move closer to the living speech of the masses.

Mao's article on the stereotypical style in the Party. Intellectuals, often, express themselves in a written language. Hence distance. This distance in the way of thinking needs to be lessened.

Theoretical, general linguistics?

[Outside, it's clouding over.]

[The little linguist, a bit on the podgy side or at any case rather plump, has a very gentle expression.]

– Linguistics: 1) teach the living language of the masses; 2) teach the classic language, assimilate what is good, living; 3) study of modern languages, what is good in them, creation of useful words. These points are being studied. Between intellectuals and vocabulary and grammar: not many differences; but what the intellectual needs to do is to share the feelings of the masses through their language. Often, intellectuals: insipid

---

* Critique of Pragmatism-Empiricism (Kant), Machianism (actually: Lenin's material).

language, empty of meaning; so through language, one learns feelings.

4) The last man, who hadn't spoken: Political Sciences, History of Chinese Revolution, etc. Courses common to all sections. He: History of Chinese Revolution under the Party leadership. Each course: specialized. – Lectures? No, now, critical discussions. – Testing knowledge? Sort of continuous assessment. If student wrong, teacher must discuss with him and help him out. Exams: not completely excluded: form they take, varies, it depends on subject: modern languages, mathematics: exam. Exams with books allowed. For certain subjects: notes (exams with closed books).
New exams: social research → composition of an overview, an article.
Emphasis on the ability to analyse and find solutions for concrete problems.
End of session 12:30 p.m.

I remember: they didn't want us to be taken to the University, explaining that we'd see libraries, laboratories: 'without any interest', 'you didn't come to China for that!'

[The essence of Chinese dress – and thus of the Chinese body: short jacket and short trousers.]

1:45 p.m. Leave hotel for the station.

It will be necessary to start off with the major fact (Phenomenology): the absolute uniformity of Clothes. The reading of the social dimension is turned upside down. Uniform isn't uniformity.

Station. We go in through a special entrance, empty. Behind the windows, massed crowds. Still accompanied by our five. Last compartment, almost empty. Clean, comfortable. Flowers at each window. Central aisle. White seat covers. We're almost alone except, at the far end, for two or three soldiers.

2:12 p.m. On the train to Nanjing

It's grey, quite chilly, feels like rain.
Entering the compartment: the eternal Disinfectant-Chlorine.
Small tables. Tea served by girl with plaits and armband.
Outside. Flat countryside. Vegetables. Summer rape. Ultimately quite French. Houses. Wheat.
Truth of the journey: China is not disorientating ($\neq$ Japan).
On the train windows, it's drizzling – it's raining.
Speed of a slow bus. Still a lot of summer rape, houses, silhouettes at work.

All these notes will probably attest to the failure, in this country, of my writing (in comparison with Japan). In fact, I can't find anything to note down, to enumerate, to classify.

Suzhou, the Chinese Venice. Rain. The train stops for a long time. Our compartment has halted next to a public urinal. Outside, Radio, extract from Beijing Opera, *Taking Tiger Mountain*.[66]

Throughout the journey, Radio programme inside the train: woman's shrill voice; music (nice tunes) and speeches, probably political.

4:05 p.m. First mountains in the misty rain.

Slowly, endlessly through the fields, the gardens very close, coming for hours on end up to the railway.

The landscape is very monotonous. It's grey, rainy, gloomy.

6:30 p.m. Night is falling. I'm reading *Bouvard and Pécuchet*.

Ph. S. and Zhao are playing Chinese chess, which I abandoned straight after asking for a demonstration.

8 p.m. Arrival at Nanjing. It's cold.

Two smiling figures from the Luxingshe, very welcoming. In a minibus to the hotel, down long avenues lined with plane trees. All this is very French.

Very nice, very comfortable hotel.

Rational, not at all exotic, not at all disorientating. We're not in Asia, from the start.

Dutch aspect of the countryside: canals, fields divided into squares, more silhouettes.

In the hotel room, always comb, brush, soap, sandals, water, and here sugar (for the black tea that will be brought the following morning).

Friday, 19 April
(Nanjing)

Didn't close my eyes, in spite of a sleeping pill, because of the hardness of the bed, a real plank.

Grey, quite chilly. Thick sweater.

As he grows more pessimistic, political lucidity seems to be returning to Ph. S.

Hotel: in a garden park, with fine essences of trees, magnolias, planes, fir trees. Very French.

Minibus. Our guides in jackets, the driver in blue. To the Great Bridge. The Young Guide's longwinded speech on Nanjing. Figures.
[Avenue of plane trees in three rows.]
When anything embarrasses them, they laugh a lot among themselves.
We are taken to the departure place on the Great Bridge, where two greet us. Small wide terrace with many flowers. Very cold wind.
Under the bridge, big piece of calligraphy engraved in gold, by Mao.
Under the bridge, passing junks in the grey.
Lower down, a crowd eyeing us up. A little girl walking on the parapet, guided by her father.

Reception office for the Bridge. Vast, frigid, Soviet-like.
'Transistorized' lift. We seem to be going up very high. But not really, as high as the upper deck, that of the car-road.[67] Under us, very close, the road goes by. A rather dashing young man goes to photograph the passing cars. It's icy cold.
Visit of the train deck under that of the cars.
Pleynet gets vertigo and I'm cold, so we both go back, while the others go to the middle of the Bridge.
Why are there two little women to control one lift?
In the icy, bare lift shaft, calligraphies as ever.
Particularly beautiful calligraphies. Always the same: the only beautiful thing; the rest: Soviet realism.

Lounge. Vast model. Sofa in front. But no tea! – Ah, yes, here it comes.

Longwinded speech by the young Functionary. Very attractive smile. Very austere jacket (like a *Polytechnique* student). Welcome.

Comrade X: explanations on the building of the Bridge.

Bridge built by the working class of China. Counting on their own strength.[68] 1960 → 1968–9. Figures, etc. Difficulties: in 1960, USSR broke the contract to provide concrete, as sabotage. So, workers: two years of experiments → special steel for construction. (Short speech.)

Other difficulties? Yes, but vague replies. No mention of the GPCR.

– Ideological difficulties of the GPCR? – Bridge built on Mao's principle, Independence and Autonomy. But also, struggles. [Endless references to Mao.] Liu Xiaoqi–Lin Biao line: trying to import everything from abroad.

[More and more, this strikes me as obvious: searchlight on the national problem (counting on one's own strength), total opacity on the social-revolutionary – which means that, at the present stage of the journey, nothing really sets China apart from a Stalinist state.]

The foundations: before the GPCR. Above: during the GPCR the Revolution gives the People considerable strength to build the Bridge.

– Role of technicians and workers? – Special steel: struggle between the lines [banal reply]. Manufacture special steel while counting on our own strength. Political practice has produced real knowledge. Many attempts are needed. Building of the Bridge: attack on the USSR.

Delightful confession: 'we're in the habit of saying Liu Xiaoqi–Lin Biao all at once.'

A gentle, long, warm handshake with the embarrassed, good-looking Presenter.
We set off again and pass slowly under the bridge.
A progressive space: a potential miniature.
Children's space. The mistake of Soviet architecture here.
After the Bridge, we get out, while the minibus turns round.
Down below, the fields of a working-class community. Green, green. An old buffalo pulls a harrow.

Back to Nanjing: first parking place of old rickshaws.
Walk round a lake – in front of the station. Swimming pool.
Fish on the ground. Narrow path between stretches of water.
Avenue of wisteria. A bit like the Bois de Boulogne, but bigger.
Wan sunshine.
Kiosks. Strollers.
We stop to take photos. Stupefied crowd.
People out boating.

Visit to the Zoo. A bit of sunshine (always in this big, lake-filled Tivoli). Like every Zoo in the world. Followed slowly by fifty people.
Panda. Double Zoo: we stare at the Panda, fifty people stare at us. (No labels.)
Often very friendly gazes, desire to say hello, to smile.
Visit to a public urinal!
They happily spit and blow their noses onto the ground.
Tigers, splendid, more beautiful than I have ever seen.
Really stripy and strong.
Monkeys. Lions. Brown bears. Huge birds of prey.
[All these animals are very big, almost grotesquely so, as if produced under pressure, or demonstrating the vigorous essence of the species.]

Disinfectant, inevitably!

Fluff from the trees floats in the air.

Birds (labels). Peacocks. Two white peacocks spread their tails.

One peacock cries 'Léon Léon' (not in Chinese?).

Among all this, swarms of children.

Visit to an exhibition (in the Park) of children's drawings and written work (at 11 a.m. before the Zoo, it was closed, they got it to reopen.)

Realistic drawings, alas! The most terrifying.

One drawing: the Nanjing Bridge in a Thermos (and two glasses). Honestly, the Thermos . . .

Politico-realistic scenes. Ping-pong. Workers at the factory. Young Red Guard. Children sowing (Back home: children loving each other). Children writing a *dazibao* on a brick wall. Schoolteacher teaching them how to write. Working-class woman reading, in the evening, by the light of an electric lamp (she is studying). Artistically, it's disconcerting.

Hairdressing (mutual aid).

Calligraphies. What a change. At thirteen, highly personal calligraphy, tending to the cursive. The drying line proves the instinctual drive behind it (you find a lot of this in Mao).

One is very beautiful, driven, grassy, cursive. In fact, it's an Grass: imitation of Mao.

Cao Next to it, very fine calligraphy, 'square' style.

Really the only form of art, and so superior.

[Three levels of perception:

1) Phenomenology: what I see. Western manner.

2) Structural: how it works: description of the operational apparatus. Stalinist level.

3) Politics: socio-revolutionary struggles. For which Revolution? Struggles between lines, etc.]

Afternoon, Nanjing Normal University

Welcome banner for *Tel Quel* (yellow on red).

Deputy director of Revolutionary Committee + other quite elderly people. An old man with a moustache, artistic-looking. Big heavily decorated lounge with vases, big tables, lanterns, flowers, Mao. Calligraphy. Perfumes.

The artist is professor at Beaux-Arts school (studied in France forty years ago), Cheng Chen Fu + Professor of Music + Professor of Education.

Speech. Welcome.

Historical overview. 1952, 11 universities [the tea is better, more golden]. Normal University: prepares secondary-school teachers. 1,600 pupils. 540 professors. 11 Universities, Sciences and arts. [The artist: he is wearing a navy blue cap, as others wear a beret and a necktie with a large bow.]

Before the GPCR, Liu Xiaoqi line, sabotage of the revolutionary line. Revisionist line: detaches education from society; creates a school with closed doors. In the course of the GPCR, we have criticized that line; have reformed in every field, methods. Now, open-door school: masses. Production. Society: union, combination. Students participate in class struggle and scientific implementation. Before: four years of study ≠ today: two and a half years. Political practice comes first. Old, foreign things: reject the bad ones, suck in the good ones. Now: less cluttered, less muddled. – Teaching method? – Relationship between teachers and students = equal; critique of education, during education; an experienced student can give a class.

Now: Pi-Lin Pi-Kong. Both: the same person, Lin Biao diehard disciple of Confucius.

[In Nanjing: appearance of dwarf trees in rounded vases.]
Back to the Rites, to Capitalism to the Past. [Pure set theme, I don't take notes.] Doctrine of Confucius: a great influence on the Chinese people. Hence [pure set theme, *ne varietur*] the campaign.

Visit. Small Physics workshop at the bottom of the beautiful garden.
[The artist was at Montparnasse, at the Grande Chaumière.[69]]
A little engine* all by itself drones away on the ground, a young Chinese man next to it.
[And what if all this country were simply: completely *naïve?*]
In a workshop (which sells electric motors for machine tools to the state), the boys are smoking.
In all these little workshops, some charming boys.
Faces often closed at first and brighten up completely with a smile if you make a sign.
[Weather still overcast.]
[The music professor has also been to France; to Nancy and Paris, where did a bit of violin and composition.]
The Library.
[The rational tablecloth has been draped over us, so incidents, folds, the absurd are rare ≠ Japan.]
Library: Mothballs.
[The two artists are charming, gentle, a bit out of things.]
Library: it's charming, clean, discreet. This University: an anti-Vincennes.[70]
Translation of Zola and Maupassant.
Bell like in school.
It's a sort of Campus.

---

* A little generator.

Beaux-Arts school: First year: 30 pupils. Second year: 120 pupils. Presentation by the Artist.

Break in a little lounge, looking at pictures by the professors: Mao inaugurating the Nanjing Bridge; a delegation with a red flag going up the ramp to the Bridge. Realistic-poster style. GPCR: open the workshops (before, always in the workshop; based on old paintings): go to the factory, to the communities and the military camps: express actions in pictures. We also provide the communities with propaganda pictures. Before, worker-peasants served us (merely as models), today: they are provided with paintbrushes.

Two styles: 1) modernized traditional Chinese with socialist content;* 2) Soviet-realist (foreign).

Caricatures (by students) Pi-Lin Pi-Kong (they're quite horrible caricatures , since they are themselves quite realistic – which is a contradiction for a caricature. Lin Biao served up with every theme, with his baldness and his rather un-Chinese appearance: his two-faced character, the genius, the Doctrine of the Mean, the dynasty (the son)). [Highly thematic language: Few themes.] Although they are made by several people, exactly the same Style.

Workshop: production by a calligraphy teacher of a long calligraphy. Drives, twists, violent dots, and elegant result. He stamps it with a red seal. All his little workbench: paintbrushes, inkwell, saucer of water.

Very quick

Another: big canvas in old style. Sort of wash drawing. He is clean, in a blue smock, with clean hands.

First year: Cartoons. Second year: Posters.

---

* For example: Vast landscape with trees, Chinese valley + cable car cables (Genre: wash drawing).

Biology (on the second floor), i.e. in fact a little Museum of Zoology and Botany.

The musician has a pair of velvet trousers and an old-style jacket, albeit in gabardine (Mandarin style). In fact, we are told, a winter jacket. You can see the ancient origin of the Mao collar.

Musique. Hall (cf. gymnastics hall), a grand piano. Pupils. Applause. Welcome.
Concert. A quartet of girls sings a welcome; on the piano a dance-like melody. It's played correctly, with ease. Pretty voices. The girls are pretty.
Solo on the Tchiba[71] (traditional violin) by a young boy on a chair. Sort of upright balalaika with plucked strings. Technically perfect. Boy with yellow face, pensive, about sixteen. Elegance.
Girls' choir. Song of Women-Pilots: very martial. Stereotypical gestures to add emphasis. In discreet counterpoint. *Pianissimi* and *crescendi*. Then: divided choir. All of this excellent; should be exported, by Lombroso![72] The girls are delightful, in spite of the drab colours. Short jacket, short trousers, plaits, Chinese shoes.

Flute solo. A boy. Cf. Panpipe. Peasant's song.
Boys' choir. Accordion. Song. Sailing by night. Very Russian. (*Crescendi*, ensemble.) Rather ugly, Tenors/Bass. Song of the Partisans.
Boy. Solo on two-stringed violin (+ piano). (Banal ritornelli by the accompanist): Very good technique. Very expressive. Instinctual drives. Eros.

Song by a girl. 'The Sun is Red.'
Big ensemble of ancient instruments. 'The soldiers and the Populace.'
The girl's feet under the xylophone:

= Well behaved: this reproduces the precision of her announcement.

Back to the lounge. Tea. Questions.
– Teaching of Chinese literature.
Ancient literature: The bad is criticized, the good is retained (*The Dream of the Red Chamber*).[73]
Modern: the characters are analysed (echo of the current 'Peasants-Workers-Soldiers' spirit).
[Stronger perfumes. Chamber pots.]
'Form serves content.'
– Painting. They learn 1) cartoons, 2) posters. No course on history (but the teachers study it. Critique of western painting). The old artist: we study Marxism, it's hard, to raise our level [it can't be helped: this old denizen of Montparnasse is a bit pitiful].
– Pi-Lin Pi-Kong campaign: yes, within the School, in all work. Confucius's influence in contemporary life: 'the leaders are intelligent, the inferiors are fools; those who study hard become dignitaries', etc. But in the campaign , at present, the emphasis is mainly on the political dimension, etc. Bricks on Lin Biao: honeyed words, red flag, two-faced, etc.

Nanjing Normal University, Friday, 19 April, 6 p.m.

24 — (Rappel de la visite de l'imprimerie et des speeches qui y furent tenus). La Doxa est très forte, faute d'un limonbage de blocs de stéréotypes; mais comme il s'agit d'une combinatoire, on peut tout de même lire, voire déchiffrer la parole (vivante, signifiante) à travers les <u>oublis</u> ou les <u>marques</u> de certains stéréotypes.

De plus: la pensée vive, individuelle (la "conscience politique", l'aptitude analytique) doit se lire dans les interstices du tissu <u>stéréotypique</u> (alors que chez nous, pour faire nouveau, échapper à la mortification endoxale, ce sont les stéréotypes eux-mêmes qu'il faut tirer).

— Avion Pékin Shangai (13h15). Boeing tout neuf — Nombreuses casquettes dans le toc américain. Les Hôtesses: le treillis kaki, les nattes, les couettes, pas de sourire; le contraire des minauderies occidentales — Pas un sourire, en n'importe quelle occasion.

— Nos Hôtesses potpourris, austères et tressées nous servent une assiette, un couteau, une poire (genre navet sucré) et une serviette chaude.

25

— Typologie des coiffures fémi-
nins  coupe dante

 natta couette
coupée ave
élastiques

 nattes
avec élastiques

14°5. Shanghai : 14° : gris et
pas chaud, qques gouttes
de pluie.
Plus chaud. Palmiers.
Mimosas. Parfums

— Accueil de 3 bleus marine
dont un rédacteur de
la Maison d'édition
de Shangha
Plus intellectuels ?
Moins touristiques.
lunettes (des variа-
tion, une typologie ?)

— Bcp de monde, plus attirant.

— Nlleuse enseigne en
pinyin (on enseigne
les déchos, paraît il)

NOTEBOOK 2

— Notebook 2 —

6 p.m. Lin Biao: To restrain oneself? To conceal oneself. Wait for the propitious moment. An arriviste, two-faced.

Lin Biao and the reading of Mao: chose quotations, phrases to be recited, instead of studying the thought as a whole, in its depth and its Marxist extension. He sheltered behind an alleged practical realism.

Carried the Red Flag so as to oppose the Red Flag. He wanted to undermine the study of Mao.

[The Artist: 69 years old: very moved when we left.] His yellowed fingers, with long fingernails.

It's raining.
Dinner.

[Ph. S. forgot to get from Zhao a 'document' that was the pure and simple list of all the 'bricks' useful for a translator: the absolute semiotic document.[1]]

Apparently they don't have any identity cards. Probably a work permit.

[No trace of an incident, a fold, no trace of a *haiku*.[2] The nuance? Drab? No nuance?]

[For a week, I haven't felt any opening up in my writing, any *jouissance* in it. Dry, sterile.]

8 p.m. *Children's show in one of the hotel lounges.*

Small audience of foreigners, Japanese, a few Chinese.

At the far end, curtain, three green plants in big rounded vases.

Spotlights. On one side, little accordionists, xylophone.

1. Little girls wearing make-up, wearing red scarves, smiling artificially. Red Flag. Little boys with make-up.
Welcome.

2. Choir of the same. Stereotyped gestures. Hands with fingers splayed.

The female presenter is taller, wearing a green skirt.

3. Flute solo by a young boy with a red cravat (he's wearing make-up).

4. Flute by a smaller boy.

5. Little red ballet of girls in boots and tunics, Russian style. Little cowgirls, they have a bucket. A guy comes on, in a blue tunic. The shepherd? Dialogue. Songs.

6. Song by a little slip of a girl, almost a baby with make-up.

7. Ballet of little girls. Gardeners. All those colours are westernized and horrible, reds, acid greens.

Vague mimicry of dance, a bit like *Coppélia* or *Giselle*.

8. Little boys sailors' collars. Mimicking sailors.

9. Scene: elements of a stage setting. Little girls. School. They're learning pinyin. Study the Revolution. They have red cheeks like on propaganda posters: health, zeal, courage, etc.

10. Ballet for girls, shouldering sacks. They dance with their thumbs sticking right out. A scene of mutual aid between washerwomen and a soldier. Solidarity.

11. Big orchestra. National instruments + two violins and a cello, an accordion.

12. Mixed chorus + two schoolboys (?) one with a ball, the other with an exercise book.

13. Pink ballet of girls around a rope with pompons. (Cf. the

number with a double rope, footwork. Garden of the Forbidden City.³)

14. Orchestra and big tubular xylophone for soloist: a very little girl. She hits the notes energetically. A sort of castrating Alice. Very Romanian.

15. Corps de ballets. Red bouquets. Tableaux vivants. Theme: all the peoples of the world. A kid in brown tracksuit and short pants over it, probably pretending to be a Negro. There's a girl from Tonkin. The ballet students arrive, little pink fleas, they don't do much and then vanish. Final basket of flowers. Group like piece of Soviet realist sculpture, in an ascending line.

9:30 p.m. The whole troupe takes its final bow.

And the troupe of hotel guests returns through the rain across the gardens; poor guys, reduced for the evening to an official show that finishes at 9:30!

Saturday, 20 April 74 ## (Nanjing)

Up at half past six. Outside it's cloudy, gloomy, drizzly, raining. However, a shrill record is bellowing away, outside. My hotel window: mosquito mesh. Fir trees, lawns, magnolias. Wall and inscription in red.

Crossing the garden at seven to the dining room. It's raining very heavily.

Postcards – a never-ending pile of them, and it takes forever, and it's a mess, a bloody pain sticking the stamps on.

Still *no* news from France for a week. The country has been rubbed out, blown away, annihilated. I ask Zhao: Any news from France? – Yes! M. Jobert has denounced the collusion of the two great powers, etc.[4] Sino-centrism.

By car to the Mausoleum of Sun Yat-sen;[5] along the avenues (we still haven't seen any streets), a blossoming of yellow and rust-red umbrellas.

Nanjing: a very great number of parks, trees, little banks of bamboos.

Mausoleum, a little outside the city. A long flagstone path going up to the blue-hued monument, the path lined with fir trees. In the background, a dark green hill, cloud-capped.

We walk up slowly: yellow, blue, green. Some Chinese with umbrellas. They smile.

Fir trees. While the others climb right to the top, I wait at the level of the first stele. It's raining gently, it's mild, it's silent, a bit stifling. Birds. Big flight of steps, blue and green with yellow patches on them.

The Fashion for yellow umbrellas. – Quite ridiculous! – If everyone had one (in France), it would make the rain less depressing.

Yellow umbrella with a blue ferrule, and bamboo shaft.

Short rubber boots.

I go back down by myself. Little grocery. I buy a popular brand of cigarettes and a little cake with jam.

Stop-off on the first floor of a restaurant. Acidulous black tea. 'No, it's not tea! It's strawberry'(?), says our guide.

Departure from the Mausoleum. Trip to a park, delicate green leaves. Visit to a monastery building. It's raining.

A bit further on, another stop-off. A room without crossbeams, empty, a convent for Buddhist nuns. All in wood. Light from leaves. Low vaults. Solitude.

Two students, on the ground, are copying the landscape of trees with a pagoda in the background. It's raining (what are they working in? oil? Yes. They come from Shanghai, they are working for themselves.).

[Remember Antonioni: 'Contemptible method and treacherous intent.'⁶]

Ming tomb.⁷ We dash noisily past it. A bit further on, still in the leafy, rainy wood, an alley of massive statues. The guide resists making us stop: 'Not of any interest.' Adjacent, at right angles, an alley of statues of big animals (horses, lions, elephants, two by two, face to face). I stay in the car while the others get out, take photos. Can't be bothered. I want the city, shops, a café.

[I don't know what it is – and I resist – looking at what presents itself as a priori *worth looking at* – something that I can't *surprise*. Theory of the *surprise* (cf. the incident, the haiku).]

Bathing softly in the mist, the grey sky, the water, the rain, the leaves, the green, the faint birdsong. Fluffy, green cotton wool.

In the big cheap store: bags, cap: jacket? No, the guide won't cooperate. A hundred and fifty people follow us at every sales counter.
Chinese chemist's. A thousand ancient drawers. Smell. Little scales for weighing.

Lunch: I take, to ward off migraine, ten little Chinese pills, which smell of camphor.

Afternoon
Primary School

Looks like a big Village School.

Arrival. Hail of applause follows us from class to class.

First floor. Lounge. Tea. Cigarettes. Table. Rather shabby. On the blackboard, *Welcome* in red. Flowers chalked up.

A girl class rep (bitch, vixen).

Historical overview. [In the corridors, a buzz of unruly noise.] 19 classes. 900 pupils. 36 teachers + crèche for 100 children. Five years of studies. Classes in politics, language, Chinese literature, arithmetic, singing, drawing + modern languages and general knowledge.

Before the Cultural Revolution, Liu Xiaoqi line, revisionist: intelligence comes first, detachment from political practice. We are training those who will continue the revolutionary Cause. But back to the revisionist line. Hence Pi-Lin Pi-Kong line. At the forefront, ideology education. We teach Internationalism, class struggle, the love of the party, effort in one's studies, discipline. We teach the activities of heroes, models. Workers and soldiers come to give classes to the pupils, to increase their political awareness: going out from the School (open school), combining theory and practice, education and society. Example: arithmetic: we invite accountants from a production team; class on invoicing: they go into the shops. Mao's 7 May directives:[8] students must acquire other types of knowledge, while studying; also: vegetable garden and workshop. For health, outside activities, sport, ping-pong, football. Medical examinations, check-ups. Morning and evening: prophylactic exercises for the eyes [next to me, a young – teacher? – the only boy: gentle and attractive]. Still shortcomings, they need to be corrected.

Age: from seven to twelve. Before seven: they are in the crèche. Most of them learn to read and write here, in the first year (but a few characters and numbers in the crèche).

Forty days of holiday summer + twenty days holiday winter.

Visit. A fourth-year class: they learn to write on model characters. Very hardworking. Paintbrush very straight. In fact, at this stage, they draw painstakingly and slowly.

Arithmetic class, fourth year. A young male teacher. Two youngsters at the blackboard = addition of fractions.

Language class third year. The female teacher at the blackboard; points to characters (words) on the board with a stick. The kids lift their hands up – *not their fingers* – and stand up to give the answer. At the back of the classroom, moral posters, Pi-Lin Pi-Kong Poems.

All classrooms windows open onto the corridor: collective decorating in the class opposite. All the classes get involved. What a din!

English class. Young male teacher. This will be the one that bitch of a class rep fancies. 'This is not a desk' in English. They go and write it up on the board.

Drawing lesson. Model on the blackboard: a Red Guard with his fist in the air, clenched.[9] Hideous! But they copy it nicely – better than me!

Nowhere do they utter a word. Teachers: simplicity, no aggression, no vulgarity, quiet authority.

Outside: little workshop for children. They are screwing together pieces of a biro. Three tables, fifteen or so per table. They're ten years old. One day per month. Very silent (perhaps our passing through).
[Outside, rain, mud, wind, cold.]
When we come back past the classes, at the press of a button, they applaud!
One class is playing: a sort of pass the slipper. Running flowers.[10]
Drum that stops them. So sweet. No hysteria. They are charming amongst themselves.
Covered play area. Five or six ping-pong tables. They're really good (they're small boys). A boyish lad invites Ph. S. to play. The others wait quietly in a single row.
They hold the bat the other way round from us

Other rooms, different games.
[This whole visit is delightful.]

Crèche. Inevitable little ballets (same as yesterday: not bourgeois, not simpering, no domination on the part of the ballerina girls over the very infantilized boys).
The story of the little coin lost in the street again.
Another crèche: plasticine around a table. Two sweet, tiny little five-year-olds play ping-pong masterfully.

Another Lounge. Tea at long table.
Orchestra in a corner.

Ballet, they are wearing make-up. Welcome.

Little Red Guards. Red Flag dances. Dumb shows and Pantomimes, probably running competitions.

In the corner, a girls' choir.

The little boy falls over. The others come back. Mutual aid. Solidarity.

[Chill in this school open to all the draughts.]

Ballet of girl militias: 'Aim at the object': caricature of Lin Biao on a placard (always depicted, alas, in the style of anti-Semitic caricatures).

[Triumphant little girls, smiling, gracious: matriarchate (afterwards, they fade away).]

And always the militant 'line'.

Songs with expression: 'We are learning to play ping-pong' (ballet).

[Oh dear, they have smiles like air hostesses.]

One girl is wounded! Mutual aid, Solidarity.

Red bows in their hair. 'Friendship first, then competition.'

Little ballet: learning how to Latinize characters.

[It's never-ending, hackneyed, and the weather's cold.]

The whole choir on benches: Song of the Red Scarf. It's a tiny little girl who, on a chair, conducts the choir. Matriarchy!

The guys (second row) are a bit left behind.

Arrival of the rest of the troupe, disguised in different

costumes from around the world. 'All children of the world, unite!'

= Final scene. The children vanish.

The teachers get together round the table. Tea. Questions and answers. All the questions blocked, to start with.

– Pi-Lin Pi-Kong at the School? We organize the pupils to study the editorial in the *Daily* and follow its guidance.[11] We critique Lin Biao and Confucius: Restrain oneself and return to the rites = to restore the slave system = to restore capitalism. Both: the same: back to the past. [It's the women, like 'lady bosses', who reply]. We organize meetings, we ask the pupils to write articles, we invite old peasants to speak about their memories of the old society. Workers-Peasants-Soldiers are invited to come here to criticize things together.

Children: they take part from fourth and fifth year. We have taken the formula Drawings and Songs for Pi-Lin Pi-Kong. The little girl, the pupils' rep, makes a remark (she is wearing a red scarf): in our school, there are things that go 'against the tide';[12] for example: in one class, two children quarrelling; a teacher solves the problem, but says that one child is better, and favours that one; but the class guards oppose this, help the teacher to correct his mistake; the children become friends. – What was this quarrel about? – It was outside class time, at football. – And the teacher happens to be here! He's a young man, charming, in blue, who served us tea. – The teacher is pleased, very happy to correct his mistakes.

[Oh the draught in the school stairwells and corridors! – Dismal weather.] [I'm freezing.]

[Some men teachers – some women teachers – one of the latter, middle-aged, who's speaking right now – have faces, eyes that

are incredibly radiant, others have slender, dreamy faces.*]
[Often have very nice teeth]
[The longwinded speeches continue. School, Family, Society,
etc. but my thoughts drift.]
Three criteria: intellectual: examination, politics, physique.
[All those questioned, and this is a constant feature, take
great trouble in answering, they don't leave out any question, but they're obviously scared stiff. It's an endurance test
for them.]
Finally, the little girl demonstrates the eye exercises – to rest
them? No, to stop yourself getting short-sighted – on meridian
points – and at the same time you can relax (in the class, five
minutes per day).
Gift presented by the girl: a biro (one of those from the workshop) and a piece of calligraphy (the same: 'study hard to make
progress every day') and a drawing.
Departure.
(I am reluctant to leave the two very good-looking ones.
Gentle, warm hands.)

In the restaurant (an endless request, finally granted!): very
cheap and cheerful downstairs, but we are told to slip upstairs
into a room with blue seats.
Dinner: hors d'oeuvre in the shape of a fish coloured red and
blue, very delicately.
Various alcoholic drinks, beer.
Warm shrimps finely chopped with a little salad.
Sichuan dish. Meat. Chilli. Pine kernels. Wonderful. Very
hot!
Sauté of chicken, bamboo shoots.

---

* Dimples.

Little fritters of duck liver. [All delicious].

Big fish in sauce, breaded, with pine kernels.

All this presided over by the Luxingshe boss, Wan, epicurean and bon vivant, who obviously loves his food.

Meatballs of something.

Soup with drawn lid. No, it's a ragout of eggs and vegetables like Swiss chards.

The rice is served last. – 'It doesn't go well with alcohol, you see.'

Soft white bread. Soup. Napkins.

Euphoria (at last).

We are going to go to the Cinema. *The Mountain of Green Pines*. Action: 1962. Initial difficulties. Liu Xiaoqi encouraged in the countryside the tendency 'Individual plots of land. Free market (kulaks?), applauded by a handful of rich peasants, right-wingers, etc. plotting to restore capitalism, etc.' (There follows the political narrative of the film by our guide Jao. Obviously: the Goody/the Baddy).

History of the Whip, symbol of Power. (Jao reads a translation.)

1974 film. It is by the director? after a novel.

Cinema. Disinfectant. In the Circle, first row. Huge place. Working-class feel. Disinfectant.

News: long sequence. Mao Boumediene.[13] Impressive/scary.

Film *sui generis*.

Sunday, 21 April
(Nanjing)

Cloudy, not warm.
We set off for the People's Commune (1 hour 20 mins by car,*
mountainous region). A bit of sunshine, wan.
No it's not mountainous. Flat countryside, attractive, well cultivated, very green. Buffalos, mauve flowers to fertilize the earth
(manure), oil-seed rape. Densely populated.

Arrival in the courtyard of the Commune. Greeting. Hall.
Table. Thermos. Tea, cigarettes, napkins. Introductions.
Longwinded speech by guy in cap. Welcome to the Tung Jin
Commune.
[The tea is less bad than elsewhere.]
Overview: Commune downstream of the Yangzi. Mainly hills.
15 production brigades + one suburb. 199 production teams (14
for silviculture, 2 for market garden fields, the rest cereals: rice,
wheat). 30,000 men.
Before the Liberation, deserted land; natural conditions bad:
floods and droughts. Limited output. Very poor lifestyle.
[On the road, always well populated, no cars, but several
lorries. A lot of porterage, scales on one's shoulders.]
After the Liberation, huge masses engaged in the organizational
and collective drive. 1950: Agrarian reform. Mutual aid groups.
Cooperatives. 1958: People's Commune. Productive forces
liberated, the People's standard of living raised.
[Outside, a wan sunshine breaks through.]
Cultural Revolution: poor peasants, zealous spirit, mobilized,
mass movement, take their example from the production

* 40 kilometres from Nanjing.

brigade of Dazhai. How? a) spirit of Dazhai, struggle against heaven and earth, b) count on our own strength, work hard, c) develop irrigation, forests, fields.[14] [All this still vague and banal.] We have changed the face of Nature: dug 8 rivers, built 200 li of canals (1 li = ½ km), 70 stations for irrigation and drainage; in the hills 11 reservoirs (of rainwater). Hydraulic projects for several years: 6 million steres of land. The natural landscape has been changed; its output has stabilized. We have created rice fields, cultivable fields. Good harvest for twelve consecutive years. 1973, cereals: 46,800,000 pounds; increase of 5½ times compared to before the Revolution; and compared to before the Cultural Revolution: 55%.

[In the yard – low brick houses – a very fine light green tree, a kind of Liberty Tree Bigger contribution to the state: 1973, contribution in grain: 20,690,000 pounds – Reserve: 11,600,000 pounds. In addition to all this: factory for repairing ploughing instruments, factory to process the grain, factory to cut stones, make bricks. Electric pump station. Ponds for fish.

All this by applying the principle: counting on our own strength. Today: 122 different tractors, 522 machines for husking rice, 374 generators, 112 motors, 3 lorries.

[All this a bit like a child's game, very Fourierist]

All mechanized or semi-mechanized.

Education and Health. Development after the Cultural Revolution.

Education: since the Cultural Revolution, 28 primary schools, 4 secondary schools = 5,600 schoolchildren, 194 teachers. All the children at school, without exception.

Health: collective health system. Hospital ↔ health centres (barefoot doctors).

[Never anything on the way wages work, the properly social, owners.]

Today: the peasants' lives improving day by day. Quite a remote region and yet 90%: electricity (some Radios and loudspeaker in every home).

All these results due to the victorious revolutionary line of Chairman Mao, to the Dazhai model.

There are still shortcomings: in the rhythm of production, mechanization, accommodation. But with the principle of Mao (counting on our strength), victory will be ours. Full stop.

Announcement of the Programme of the visit.

11 a.m. We go out for the Tour. Nice weather.

Repair machine workshop. Some fifteen workers.

Workers in muffs and caps. Boy with his hair sticking up. Bench in the yard.

Workshop for processing cereals. Noodles arriving on little bamboos.

Refinement of flour. A big machine, deliberately trembling.

Polishing of rice: husking: from yellow to white.

Cereal reservoirs (rice):

Commune Hospital (a sort of dispensary, really horrible).

Little exhibition of Chinese plants, in little saucers, roots, seeds, dried mushrooms, tubercles, etc.

A little soldier with a big smile holds a swollen baby doll by its overall.

Shops for technical objects.

The hairdresser. The bookshop. I buy a poster: 'The army

and the people are the same family' (soldier entering peasants' home).

Tour of shops (small purchases).

Nice weather.

Break in the first room: warm napkins (huge, rural).

Rustic lunch. Bare little room. Two round tables in waxed wood. About eight pots. Beer. Noodles, rice (at the end). Chicken (boiled, whole), Fish with brown sauce. Balls of fish-eggs (like quenelles), etc.

It's nice, but rustic (the chicken is tough).

Break in the room. Tea.

Visit to a house. Clean. Glasses brought out of a cardboard box. Tea.

Posters and cartoons on the wall + Mao.

The house, in the midst of the rice fields. Grandfather with ancient jacket. Dog. A sewing machine.

History of the family by the father. Set theme: the past.

The house belongs to him, but was built by the Commune's construction team (a sort of tax of 12 yuans to the Commune when construction is complete). Now, houses built in a line along the road. There's a plan. The house cost him 900 yuans. Possible loans from the brigade or the production team – not from the Commune. Would still like: a clock, watches, clothes and two extra rooms.

Work? There are norms. The work of each team rotates.

What does the girl want to do in life? – She'd like to work for her living in the countryside, but it's the state which decides.

[In one room, a small amplifier on the wall.]

[In short, always and everywhere, they're angels! For relaxation, she studies, etc.]

Back to the hall. [Horribly tired, saturated. Sleepy.]

Arrival of two young people, a boy and a girl (barefoot doctor) + a third (schoolteacher). All this for the Discussion(!). I'm worn out.

Questions (asked all at once).

[The boy, young, with yellow crystal glasses, has very slender hands.]

Replies: Brick: know the Party line, get the Peasants to know it, etc.

[In spite of the words 'struggle', 'effort', etc. what angelism!*]

[I lose track, too tired. This seems completely banal to me.]

Revisionist Liu Xiaoqi line: the *sanziyibao* (extension of individual plots of land, etc.) [Sort of NEP]: back to capitalism.[15] Opposition from the peasants.

Then, revisionist line of Lin Biao: slandered our progress.

[We almost want to get them to give us *concrete* examples of lines in their commune, their experience, etc. But they are always evasive; it all remains a matter of generalities, or at least it doesn't get beyond themes valid for every commune, etc. They can't give concrete examples of opposition between lines; and no wonder! The 'line' is a purely verbal entity, an abstract complex of themes – next to which, no doubt, unchanging, their lives continue! . . .]

Example: how Lin Biao undermined production: every day they had to issue instructions in groups 'to be faithful to Mao', in front of his portrait, this was a waste of time.

Wages, to each according to his abilities, to each according to his work. Every day, to each, *points* for work, depending on work: at the end of the year, they are handed out.

---

* Rather: idyllism.

A production team: very varied. The biggest 200 to 300 people. Average: 150 people.

A brigade: 3,000 people or 1,000 people, it varies.

Work-points: depending on quality and quantity (the norms). There's a production committee which sets the norms.

[It drags on. Nobody is very enthusiastic.]

Lin Biao had decreed the principle of the three Fidelities: to Mao, to his thought, to his line → Ceremonial observation of this principle morning and evening, with a report (i.e. examination of conscience). Cf. *supra*.[16]

We leave the Commune at 3 p.m. Nice weather.

A lot of people on the roads and in the streets of Nanjing: shops full to bursting. It's Sunday.

In the Friendship Shop. Even uglier than elsewhere – and empty (it's on the first storey) while at ground level, a delightful swarm of activity. Nothing to buy.

5 p.m. We go back to the hotel. I'm dead tired, slept.

[The *daʒibao* – numbered – are discussed beforehand in the cell. There were free ones only after the Cultural Revolution]

[One of the possible meanings of the Pi-Lin Pi-Kong campaign: destroy the cult of personality.]

[The Commune official, rather disquieting; the demeanour of a real leader, a boss – and probably powerful.]

[Huge matriarchate. Presence, extent of the mother. The girls are *shown* (≠ North Africa). The little boys crushed.]

[No trace of folklore – in the ballets, in the houses: no embroidery, etc.]
[Profound absence of religion]

[Factories: Proletariat as strong core. Leading force. Absorbing problems.

Peasants. A pain in the neck. Schools: islands of sheep-like conformity. Teachers: made to feel guilty.
In short, a grid of impressions that conforms to the orthodox view.]

[Waiting for the night train to Luoyang (at Midnight), gathering in Pleynet's room, whisky, coffee, cigar and Haydn-Handel]
A bit under the weather. Slight pain in heart. It is midnight. We're about to leave the deserted hotel.

Nanjing Station. Very modern. Our minibus goes straight onto the platform via a gate that they open up for us. Deserted platform.

Monday, 22 April
(from Nanjing to Luoyang)

Good night in the sleeping car. Though still feeling queasy. It's comfortable, but we're alone. Pillows of rice.
Wakening: Flat landscape, hazy sunshine, dry, beige-pink earth, delicate green fields. Lines of trees. We enter Henan.

[Bad dream: Patrice and Roland were not in the least interested in my return. Only Évelyne showed any sympathy . . .]

Countryside: it's very French (the Beauce), but the colours are very, very delicate. And still this incredible absence of disorientation.

Breakfast in the restaurant car. We hesitate and can't decide whether it's tea or coffee.

Frequent nasty smells. Manure, cabbage, etc.

Odd the way we are completely mothered by the Agency.

Little very western stations, poor and peaceful.

On the platform, they pass along on the way back from buying a pancake-fritter before getting back on board the train.

A landscape without a fold.

The landscape isn't culturalized (apart from the cultivation of the earth): nothing that speaks of history.

We're really stuck in this special compartment (blue, lace, and thermos): no right to go for a beer in the restaurant car that's next along and empty, they bring it to us; and you have to get them to open the toilets for you every time you need to go for a piss.

The landscape is getting dryer and dryer.

Drab country.

Excellent lunch in the restaurant car. Dishes in different colours: a dark red (fish with tomato), a pale black-green (mushroom), a white-green (peas and a mysterious vegetable), etc.

Zhao's phrase, when we express any desire: 'We'll see to that' (in a warlike tone and if it were simply a matter of arranging the thing – and not deciding it). But what is definitely always fulfilled: my smallest wishes and tastes: for the children in the School to give me a page of handwriting, for me to eat a spicy dish in Luoyang, to have peonies in my room, etc.

Mao likes red chilli; he powders his dishes with it.

One possibility for a text on China would be to *sweep* across it, from the most serious, the most structured (the burning political issues) to the subtlest, most futile things (chilli, peonies).

Around 2 p.m. Broad valley with banks of dry clay, very light with holes for cave-dwellers. In the background, a carpet of wheat, little vegetable gardens with delicate plants, trees with mauve flowers, half-lilacs, half-wisteria.
Too tired to note the continuation of the lovely countryside, with its delicate trees.
Luoyang: 3 p.m.

Luoyang

Weather very fine, warm, thunder in the air. Three mute natives on the platform. Minibus on the platform. To the hotel.
Small lounge. Welcome. Programme.
Weird hotel; every room has a big lounge, but the shower is decrepit, smells of disinfectant, Morocco, stone.
'We want to visit the Temple of the white horse.' – Ah, it's being repaired![17] F. W. is furious.
Shower.

Exhibition of Peonies, the local flower.[18] A big roundabout. Everyone around us stares at us.
The purple Peonies are of no interest, but the pale-pink, white ones are wonderful (all drooping a bit in the stormy five o'clock atmosphere).
Tour through the Park. The people are nice, smiling. We cross a small hanging bridge.

At the far end of the Peony Park, tombs of the Western Han (2000 BC). A little girl does a sales pitch.

Stifling. Waited for the others outside the tomb, as well as a hundred and fifty people. Lovely weather. Peonies.

Oh no! Another Han tomb! This one: Eastern Han. Still, I go down into it, it's cooler. 1900 BC. Without exactly simpering, the young girl speaks with exaggerated diction.

Kid girl (and her mother)

City, very peaceful light.

Excellent food in the hotel.

Dinner: Zhao eats apart from us, separated by a screen and keeping up the dialogue with his back turned to us.

First news from the world: Julia has picked up the American news in Russian.

Outside the dining room, where we are alone, a big garden with peonies, a pond, a swimming pool. Three young men are practising basketball, they smile at us. We go for a stroll, go out into the avenue and are drawn by a big open-air screen in a space between modern HBMs.[19] They're showing (it's dark) an apparently Romanian film. Two young girls offer us their chairs. It's mild, like a June evening, a lot of people, it's relaxed.

The first town that doesn't feel artificial. On the way back, we walk past a group of street boys, sitting on small chairs in the avenue, playing cards; they smile at us.

A little rice alcohol between ourselves in a hotel room. But I'm exhausted and go to bed at 9 o'clock.

Tuesday, 23 April
(Luoyang)

Slept well (excellent bed and little pillow) from nine until five o'clock. But still have bad migraine – yet again. Outside, it's overcast but not gloomy. Concert of car horns and loudspeakers at six o'clock.

[One of the great features of this journey will have been: my almost daily bad migraines: fatigue, absence of siesta, food, or more subtly: big change in routine, or even: more serious resistances: *revulsions?*]

At seven a.m., washed and dressed, I'm already – or still – exhausted.

Breakfast: cakes, crêpes!

8 a.m. We set off in minibus for the caves of Longmen:[20] the sun rises. The weather is lovely, spring-like, invigorating, peaceful.

A woman from the Agency who speaks French joins up: so there are four of them.

The first thing that needs to be said about China is that there are many plane trees. Frenchness.

En route, in the town: a group of girls in the street. Swedish gymnastics in chorus. (It's the gymnastics for young people.) The old people do Chinese gymnastics, slower, more supple, more mysterious: individual gymnastics, as opposed to collective gymnastics.

[Zhao's inevitable proverbs: Chinese gymnastics: for body and mind. My preference: *mens fada in corpore salop.**]

Ch.: Not at all the type of body I like: too brusque and too hysterical (with a French elocution, full of precious idiomatic turns of phrase, that sounds hysterical).

[Make a list of the X stereotypes (bricks) that I have gathered]

Always heavy traffic on roads, very far out in the countryside, cyclists, carts, pedestrians, lorries. Driving in a stop-start, exhausting way. Predominance of vegetables in the items transported.

Longmen Caves

We turn off the road and go down along the Yi-He river, wide, gleaming.

On the banks of the Yi-He, halt, welcome house. Lounge, tea, cigarettes. Transparent blue curtains. Short introduction to the Longmen Caves. A young man gives a longwinded speech. Historical facts and figures, number of caves, statues, etc.

Several pieces of calligraphy. [Oriental perfume]

'All these [Buddhist] works represent the workers' talent and wisdom.' Very important teachings. Theft by American imperialists (Museums in New York, and Kansas): crimes.

[It's three little guys who take part in the presentation]

90% of the statues limbless and headless.

After the Liberation, caves properly protected [brick: the adverb 'properly']. Office for Protection and Direct Action of

---

* Barthes's parody of a well-known Latin phrase. His version means: 'a dull mind in a slutty body' (Tr.)

the Council for State Affairs. Budget for repairs. These arts: in the service of the People. This is the overall idea.

Nice weather, people on the bank.

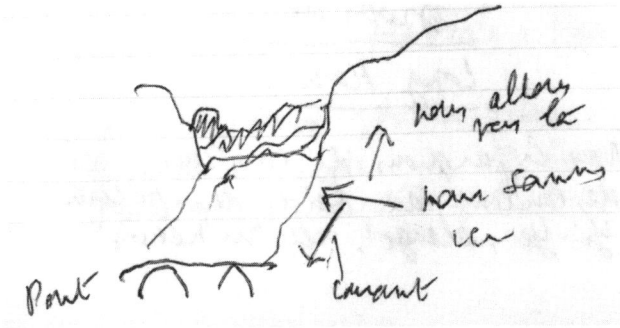

We walk along the bank, many people still walking along with us.

Lined with a thousand Buddhas inlayed into the wall like a wallpaper pattern.

Flight of steps above the first cave.

Second cave. Big Buddha at the far end and, again, a hundred thousand little Buddhas hammered into the wall. (Shallow caves: more like recesses.)

[The brick keeps appearing in the futile relaxed tone of ordinary conversation: Zhao: 'Shame that the American imperialists stole those stones' (it's a natural epithet).[21]]

[They're often pimply – and nice.]

The rock riddled with small recesses, at every level.

[If I lag behind (as often) there's always one who stays behind with me.]

Third cave. In my opinion, beautiful, tall statue at the far end, very majestic. Face scrunched up (like that of a schizophrenic's doll).

[And with all this, I won't have seen the willy of a single Chinese man. And what can you know about a people, if you don't know their sex?]

What calm (as I often wait for the others outside, being unable to look at an objet d'art for long)! Sun rather hazy, mild air. People sauntering along the sunlit riverbank. On a spit of sand in the distance, framed by the horizon, some boys; one wades out into the water, his trousers rolled up.

[Rare case of petty police-repression; one of the agency officials (already a cop in his costume) tells off – with a certain degree of anger, it seems – the nice, mild-mannered cyclists naïvely forcing their way through the gaggle of sacred tourists (us); he forces them to get off their bikes.]

Climb up steps in the rock, with fifty persons following us.
At the top, a big terrace, nicely laid out, a lot of people there already.
A real circus with seven or eight big statues, a big Buddha in the middle.
Statues: completely Chinese faces.

All of this heavily restored – after the Liberation (it's the remains of a Temple).
[The guide insists on explaining everything to me. There's a smell of food on his breath.]
As soon as we want to get by, they move right out of our way.
They take a lot of photographs of each other. As soon as they have cameras it will be awful, like the Japanese?
Relationship with the image?
Floating pricks beneath floating clothes (of workers).
Where do all these people come from, to this purely tourist site?
No village, nothing in the neighbourhood. And they're here as tourists to see us, not the site or the statues.

More steps. Cave in the middle: the oldest. Calligraphic tablets inlayed in the wall, on the ceiling. On that statue (at the far end), badly damaged, a few colours, very faded rust, washed-out blue.

The steps go up quite a way. Down on the riverside, they are waiting. The horizon, from this bend, wide open: there's no more valley, practically. It's more overcast but there's a gentle breeze. A small empty boat on the river which is quite narrow, poor, silted up. In the distance, a tight group of workers from the fields (always in compact groups. People's Communes.) Horrible smell of urine.

I'm ahead, on the upper platform, alone with a little girl, pretty and unassuming, with plaits and flat shoes over white socks.

Down on the ground, two basket carriers are washing their feet in the brickwork ditch that runs alongside the road.

[Ph. S., too, proceeds by *campaigns* – and it's tiring: from one period to the next, he always bangs away at the same old theme, with variations of examples in support, jokes, etc.: at present it's: Lacan as a henchman of religion, idealist, etc.]

The others don't come. I've climbed up for no reason, but the view, if not the cave, with a badly damaged statue, was beautiful.

Little cave: ordinances on the wall against madness (= 'the confused words of demons').

It's overcast-stormy.

We return. Very old guy with a small goatee, a walking stick and a cap.

[Remembering yesterday evening's incident, the discovery, unanticipated, of the open-air cinema, so richly incongruous (the Romanian film, the chairs brought up, the mild evening): this seems to prove that it's the continual presence, smooth as a tablecloth, of Agency officials that blocks, forbids, censors, rules out the possibility of the Surprise, the Incident, the Haiku.[22]]

10:45 a.m. Back to the Welcome House. The others buy pieces of calligraphy (copies from the caves); but they're too expensive: 300 yuans for a series, you can't take individual ones – it's 'to study calligraphy'.

Argument over the price, for we're really surprised. But it's not a picture, it's a piece of cultural heritage for study, and it's very difficult to make the copies (scaffolding, etc.). The lads are furious that we are so surprised.

In China, there's an association for Buddhism: for studying the Buddhist religion (but Specialists).

Follow up the discussion with the official. During the Cultural Revolution, it was possible to visit. No ultra-leftist demonstrations.

This acts as a lesson for the children: how the imperialists stole, etc. . . .

On the other side of the river: More caves. You get a good view of the ones we've just come from; the big one, like an amphitheatre, is superb. The rest looks like a dovecot.

Easy road. I walk up a bit, leaving the caves behind.

Sign in Russian and English: foreigners are forbidden to go past these limits.

Military lorries drive past frequently. That must be the reason.

Intensely noisy squeal of carts that could be heard from the other side (Mules, little horses, donkeys).

[Shocking incident of the calligraphies that were too dear: probably, Buddhism can be studied, but not spread. Perhaps also full of Confucian formulae.]

Back in the jolting minibus: at the (tiresome) bidding of Ph. S., inevitable revolutionary songs (including especially the Internationale). And we drive past a procession with a red flag.

The woman guide: she earns 56 yuans per month, her husband technician the same; they are cadres; for the daughter's kindergarten: 10 yuans per month.
Workers: eight categories of wages, from 40 to 100 yuans per month (experienced worker). Average: 60 yuans per month. Accommodation costs?[23]

Lunch: look, it's French fries!
Another discussion in which Ph. S., as relayed by Pl., absolutely has to denounce Buddhism as religion, idealism, political power, etc. Voltaireanism. But the problem, the only one, is Power. And every system is compromised by power – including this one.

Afternoon *Tractor factory*

[On the way there: skill of our driver who amazingly just manages to avoid a young cyclist.]

Welcome to the Factory: a dozen people, young workers: one main character with a slender face and the dark suit of an official. Big Lounge, armchairs, tea, four portraits, painting of a fir tree in the old style.
Very rhetorical welcome. Overview by the assistant director of administrative affairs (young).
This factory: 'The East is Red' Tractor Factory.
1955, completed 1959. 1,450,000 square metres, 23,000 workers including 6,700 women.
[It's wealthier, bigger, more developed: more serious]

Built with the support of the USSR in Stalin's day. But 1957, Khrushchev started going against Marxism-Leninism and proletarian internationalism. The USSR tore up the contracts, recalled the experts, stopped providing materials, so as to crush in its cradle the Chinese tractor industry. Experts recalled in a single night.

[Opposite me two young little workers, charming, listen closely.] [The tea is nice, golden.]

A great number of difficulties, losses.

[In the lounge there are fifteen from the factory listening to their comrade and participating with their smiles.]

Examples of losses caused by the withdrawal of Soviet support. Indictment of the USSR continues (unusually long and detailed).

[Clear distinction between Stalin and Khrushchev: it was *this* USSR which has broken with them, and which he condemns, and not Stalin's. Khrushchev has introduced and 'created' revisionism and imperialism.[24]]

The USSR, in addition, has increased its prices, passing off worn-out pieces as new ones. All this happened in 1959–60–61, especially when Khrushchev came to power.

Also: revisionist line of Liu Xiaoqi: profits from the order, material stimulation. This enabled us to produce tractors of one type only.

Proletarian Cultural Revolution by the light of Chairman Mao's revolutionary line: independence of the economy and counting on our own strength; we have extirpated the influence of the Soviets and Liu Xiaoqi.

We have organized the triple Union(?) expert workers . . .[25]

Series of reforms on production, technology, and equipment. Now, we manufacture four types of tractors: 75 hp + caterpillar-track tractors + 60 hp bulldozers + 50,000 kw generators. – And above all, GPCR: a 40 hp tractor with tyres that suits the needs of our countryside best. Every year, currently 21,500 tractors.

Factory managed by the Party. Just two grades:

1) Revolutionary Committee of the Factory in general +

2) Branches of Revolutionary Committee (17) (= Workshops).

Factory Hospital, 350 beds. Kindergarten. Crèche. Five primary schools. Library. Floodlit sports stadium. Swimming pool.

[All these 'workers' have clean, slender hands.]

Visit:

[As everywhere else the toilets are divided into Gentleman/ Ladies*.]

It's a whole town.

Vast hall. Hammers. Furnaces. Heat. Vulcanian. Terrifying bangs, incandescent bars being pounded. Handsome Workers. They stop their work and gather in groups to watch us pass by.

[I try to stay by the most attractive one, but what's the use?]

Another hall. Forges.

The workers' faces are gentle, open, nice and serious, smiling. This is the People at its most obviously lovable.[26]

In another corner of this city, women's workshop. Small pieces. A few men. They are scratching away at the pieces (moulds).

[All this: very much a lesson in things.]

[Barefoot doctors and also workers with clean hands.]

Drying hall. Strong heat.

[The attractive one smiles to me, but what can I say? Total opacity. The timid, blushing worker.]

For the minibus trips to the factory, the retinue of fifteen people gets into another minibus.

---

* In English in the original (Tr.)

Rolling hall: twenty caricatures of Lin Biao (a dead man!).
Lift.
Workshop for precision pieces.

[A bit shameful to be strolling around as tourists among these alienated workers at their labour.]

I look at the workers more than at the pieces. And I'm basically quite right.
My worker has very slanting eyes and a bit of a moustache. He looks sixteen, but a few white hairs. He's one of the two pals in the lounge.

etc. Visit follows: etc.
Assembly line hall. On the long assembly belt, the red tractor gradually takes shape, and finally emerges in full armour, headlights gleaming. A man climbs on board and drives it out.
All this, a grand demiurgic spectacle.
Another belt of little tractors. One rolls off and starts up.
Ph. S. is invited to drive it.
Some workers come over to see. The assembly line is broken!
On an esplanade, demonstration: the tractor going crazy, pivoting on its tracks, etc.
Back to the Lounge. Break. Tea. Napkins.

Questions (in groups) and discussion:
'We have broken the blockade organized by Khrushchev's revolutionary clique and that of Liu Xiaoqi.' In our factory, one trend wants to get back to revisionism: back to profit as material stimulus; but the workers reject this.
At our last CCP Congress, Mao taught that throughout the period of socialism, there are contradictions and class struggle.

In collusion with the imperialists, modern revisionists and reactionaries, Lin Biao created an anti-revolutionary anti-Chinese movement. Lin Biao two-faced: undermined the Party's victorious line. Advocated the superiority of the intelligent, the view that heroes create history; should restrain oneself and 'return to the rites' with the aim of transforming socialist China into a semi-feudal and semi-colonial country.

An experienced worker can bear witness to the problem. [He just happens to be there! and is eagerly getting ready to take over and launch into his lecture; off he goes . . .]

The biographical story of the experienced worker: at the age of thirteen, worker for the capitalists, fifteen hours per day, treated badly; was like a slave. [Set theme of the Past.] [There are, in a complete script – and this huge factory can afford it – certain 'roles': the old worker, the old rickshaw puller, the model-mother, etc. Copy up the list in these notes.] His family, his children. His life is very happy. Over 200 yuans per month(?). Particular attention shown by the factory for experienced workers. [The old man is so keen to deliver his lecture that he gets heated and interrupts the translator.] We are also educating the young workers. Socialism alone can save China. Capitalism is the root all evils.

– The trend to get back to profit is mainly among the Young people? – That's why the old ones educate the young ones.

(Experienced workers = old workers.)

[The worker is really being put on display.]

– The Triple Union?* Experienced workers as the centre, main force + technicians + officials. New organization: management of the business. After Charter of the Iron and Steel Society and the Cultural Revolution.

---

* Cf. *supra*, the overview.

– What about young workers? Can also be experienced.

[The young friend of the Attractive guy is involved as a Young Worker of the 8th category.]

Triple Union: also at Workshop level.

Categories of workers (eight). 1. Apprentices (3 years), 2nd category, etc. (different wages) → 8th category (102 yuans) ≠ the young: 38 yuans (2nd category). The highest wage in this company: general engineer: 270 yuans. (The general engineer: either a technician sent by the state (Technical School), or a worker trained in the factory (which has its own schools).) Average wage for the factory: 54 yuans.

The Women take part in the Pi-Lin Pi-Kong movement, as victims of the old society of Confucius and Mencius;[27] Confucius despised women. Then Li Biao: oppresses, despises, exploits, women. Women: overwhelming hatred for old society, Confucius and Li Biao.

Example: Lin Biao advocated that woman could be a good housewife, prevented women from taking part in political activities. So they want to refute completely, radically Confucius and Lin Biao. Throughout this fiercely feminist speech, the row of gentle young men remain huddled and silent in their armchairs. Women have become vanguard in this movement.

Revolutionary committee (of the factory in general): 50 members, including 17 permanent.

Invitation to have dinner with the workers. Handing over of insignia from the Luoyang Factory.

Dinner in the canteen. Hatches, some fifteen or so old cooks in white behind them. 'Old Chinese'. F. W. and I go to a table where there are already two young workers, very clean, slender hands (are they 'repairmen'?), very nice. Several dishes, tasty, a bit cold, no rice, steamed bread. They eat, both quality and quantity are good; the food is nice and abundant.

Final effusions with the two nice workers in very clean blue.

At the dining room exit, two basins of lukewarm water – a sort of mouthwash – and two clean towels.

We are applauded by the whole corps of cooks (including an attractive Mongol) whom we go over to thank, and by all the workers in the canteen, standing. Outside to go to the minibus, all the cooks in a row.

And suddenly the Attractive guy shows off the bit of French that he learned at a Teacher Training School! (He actually has a nice accent.)

Back to the Lounge (more questions).

To eat like this every day, 17 yuans per month. Savings at the Savings Bank: to help the Revolution. 1 pound of eggs = 70 fens.

Alienation of the repeated movements in the assembly belt? – Those who always work on the same section: very rare. Every worker masters several sorts of section. [Feeble reply.]

[It's true that the portion of the assembly belt looks complex enough to represent a certain variety.]

[More questions, but I can't be bothered, since the replies are always idyllic.]

'*Critique of Gotha*, in particular, + *State and Revolution* + *Imperialism*,' etc.:[28] these in particular are the works studied in relation to Pi-Lin Pi-Kong.

100% of workers take part in the political and ideological study groups.

Thanks (7:15 p.m.).

'Please convey the greetings of our factory to the workers of France'(!).

The attractive French-speaker holds my hand (his is moist) for five minutes.

Evening
Local opera. Troupe from Henan

'The shops towards the sun'. The story takes place in 1963: a nice girl, she's a doughty militant. Her father, nice but in need of enlightenment, and a wicked capitalist. This illustrates 'the contradictions within the people' (around the theme of the free market).

Big hall, chock-a-block. At the last minute, we are ushered forward to our places in a line, still surrounded by the Agency.

Actors: horribly made-up, almost masked: the actors have a fat, flabby, effete physique; the women are smiling and decisive (this is very like an American matriarchy).

The make-up: rosy-cheeked for the goodies, greenish for the traitor. Cf. Ancient Theatre.

The orchestra is on the stage behind a wire mesh. On each side of the stage there are vertical lit tableaux where every so often some text appears. (But, I think, not very Brechtian.)

Dialogues and they each regularly sing their little song. American comedy.

They have very clean clothes, 'purpose-made'; nothing is wrinkled, living, 'real'. It's not Brechtian.

Second scene: inside the house: Thermos! Later on, the heroine, a travelling saleswoman, will bring a peasant – what? A Thermos!

[For this country, two sorts of pertinence: 1) Gaze of Bourgeois democracy: Peyrefitte, admiration for the state, Efficiency, condemnation of indoctrination;[29] this point of view can be adopted and maintained *before* coming here. Coming here doesn't change anything; 2) Gaze from within socialism; debates: bureaucracy, Stalinism, power, class relations, etc. The opacity remains.]

The audience is obviously just after a good laugh; great reserves of sensibility, attention, freshness, in them: they wait with intense expectancy for talent, the good old Comedy; what they are presented with is a load of rubbish that clearly leaves them with nothing to do. What a mess, what a waste! The lack of talent is a crime against the Revolution.

The actresses: highly coded movements (especially in singing). What code? Got it! movements (arms and hands, position of the feet) are those of waxwork models in the display windows of second-rate shops.
Each act ends in a Tableau vivant (diagram of the 'forwards').
Cf. the Pregnant instant[30] (here: the movement forwards).
Religious: the gesture of domination of the Good Man over the Demon. (Here: the Woman walks on the man's head.)

Wednesday, 24 April (Luoyang)

Overcast, like yesterday. – Daily migraine.
Breakfast: omelette with noodles. Meat fritters. French toast (delicious), big cake like a Saint-Honoré gateau.

Yesterday. The Show: the Positive Hero always seems to be a Woman (young girl or old woman, no 'Woman of Thirty').[31]

8 a.m. Pack my bags. The sun rises.

Visit to a factory for mining operations
We are, as usual, awaited on the steps.

Lounge, tea, etc.

Welcome in the name of the Revolutionary Committee.

= Factory of Machine-Tools for mines.

Short overview by the director of administrative affairs for the Revolutionary Committee. Serving the coalmining, and iron and steel industries. 10,000 people.

[Here the armchairs are in leather, the lounge is not very big. Four portraits + Mao. Outside the weather is nice, wonderful.] Sorting, washing of the ore. [Dark tea.] Description of the machines (I leave this out). [The tea is nice, perfumed, not insipid.] Factory built under Stalin. Then Khrushchev, recall of experts, damage to production (familiar Set Theme). So, count on our own strength.

[Draw up a list of the Set Themes: assemblage of bricks, example: Set Theme of Past/Present, Set Theme of Broken-Contract.]

Hospital, etc. (150 beds.) Club* for 1,000 people.

Secondary School (2,000 pupils) + 4 primary schools (3,000 children) + 7 kindergartens. Cinema twice a week. Free showers.

change of Female workers: 28%. Same wage as Men.
pen Politics: women equal to men. Daily life: favours (childbirth 56 days paid leave, breastfeeding one hour per day).

After the Cultural Revolution, development of production. At present, Pi-Lin Pi-Kong, to promote production. Now, greater activity on the occasion of 1 May.

Visit.

[Yesterday Opera: We are *sacred*: people come up in crowds to stare at us, they move aside so as not to touch us.]

---

* Club = leisure.

Great Hall. The workers stop working and stare at us. Brilliant steel, soaked, filings.

[Summary so far: description of language: dare to do it. Conclusion: *needs help*. So the sole correct position: *friends*, travelling companions.] (Find Mao quotation in *Red Book*.[32]) No eros, here.]

A small man next to me, his eyes staring into space, turns out to speak a bit of French (one year at the French Institute of Tendou.[33] Cf. the man yesterday).

Notice-board.

Caricatures Pi-Lin Pi-Kong.

Big gateway (painting) by Comrade Tiu Yu Lou[34] – heroic (?): used to work in this workshop (shop foreman) [surrounded by fifty workers]: a very good worker. Went off among the destitute peasants to educate them: the village of Lan Kao became a good village for him = 'Good pupil of Chairman Mao'.

Poster: longwinded piece on the Paris Commune (103rd anniversary): Great Proletarian Festival, Pi-Lin Pi-Kong Movement: 18 March 1871: First Red Power in the World. Supported by Marx.[35]

[A lot of them stare at us, gather round us. A good opportunity not to give a damn! No cadences?]

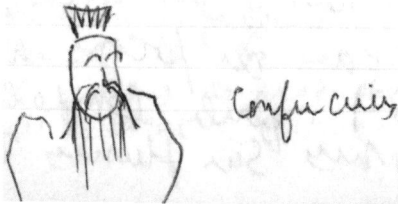

Confucius

Big picture. Photos relating to the Hero. Reliquary of objects: his jacket, his desk, his scarf, his bench, etc.

Another, small, guy speaks French.

Another Hall. Pictures. Caricatures (this time with an attractive piece of calligraphy, nice and grassy). – No, actually it's a cartoon, with different episodes.

[The woman guide, who is thirty and looks fifty, is very anxious about the correctness of her phrases. But I give her five out of five and she brightens up.]

Brick: 'Poor and medium-poor peasants'.[36]

'He goes into the countryside to work with ———— (brick).'

Theme: intellectuals in the countryside.

Behind us (we decipher the tableau filled with workers' poems): compact crowd of workers in several rows.

We pause more in front of the Pictures than in front of the machines. We are beings of language.

'I'm always the last (in the line).' – Because you're old, the amiable guide with her correct phrases tells me.

Hall. Forges. Rolling mills.

Quieter workshop. A dozen workers at one table stare at us 'sitting doing nothing'.[37]

Another Workshop. On the edge of the central aisle, two workers sitting on pieces, the one gently encircles the other's wrist in his hand, plays with it, very softly. Innocence?

This is the most relaxed factory, where they have the most breaks. (I translate, in the final round of thanks, congratulating them on the calm and control of the effort they put in.)

Back to the Lounge. – Questions?

We scarcely have any.

(It's 10:30 a.m.)

The production norms are set by the state.

Classic arrangement of a Welcome Lounge:

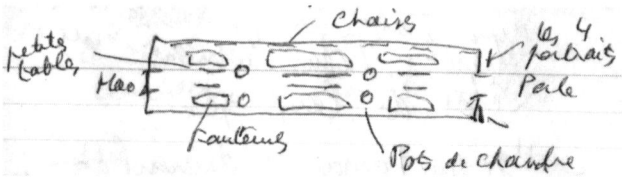

Triple alliance: Workers, Officials, Technicians.

Revolutionary Committee of this factory: 32 people, on the principle of the triple alliance (old, middle-aged, young). In order to make an election, discussions at factory level: candidates of every sort, vanguards of the GPCR: once discussed, ratification and approval by higher echelon, by Party Committee and Municipality of Luoyang.

Revolutionary Committee: experienced cadres, young women (4) + workers + technicians. How much time? Depending on circumstances, concrete conditions in the company. Right of dismissal by workers. Current Committee: September 1967. Current Pi-Lin Pi-Kong campaign? No changes, but new members (the vanguards that are appearing). There are Party members, and Party non-members.

Revolutionary Committee and Morals? Has at its disposal the Administrative Bureau, which looks after marriage (the Trade Union looks after decease) (the Administrative Bureau: small affairs ≠ Revolutionary Committee: big affairs). Marriage: the young formulate their desires, the Administrative Bureau approves and sends back to the District for the formalities (government). Then, Administrative Bureau: gives accommodation, furniture, etc. Date fixed by the couple (days off, Sundays), participation of their comrades. A few days' holiday.

– In which case is there negative reply? – Marriages late in life; a rule respected voluntarily. So in general no refusals.
– What do you expect concretely, here, from the Pi-Lin Pi-Kong campaign? – After the Cultural Revolution, right-wing trend that neglected the achievements of the Cultural Revolution. The present movement refutes this trend. Tendency to favour material stimulation: this is what we criticize.
End. Handing over of insignia.
Julia's last question: Divorces? Very rare.

Hotel. In the hall, two boys sitting down: one has his arm round the neck of the other, who holds his hand in both his hands [but alas, most of the time they have very moist hands].

Note: a president of the Revolutionary Committee: 240 yuans per month.

Bring out clearly the uniformity of clothing, but also its implacable subtle differentiation (cadres/workers/functionaries). In fact, unlike what I had noted down, it's the structure of the uniform (homogeneous but with marks).

Confucius: King Zen. But this is actually honorific (like Laozi). So today, on the radio, people say Kong (Shiu, the old?), or Konfuss.[38]

Story of the worn-out Bic I try to get rid of, hiding it away right at the back of a drawer, and which comes back to me three times.[39]

The train for Xi'an is late; we wait first in the hotel, then in a waiting room at the station: tea (without cigarettes), armchairs with white covers. Portrait of Mao alone (without the four others). Calligraphy. It's 3:20 p.m.

Solemn thanks of the plump head of the Agency.

On the train from Luoyang to Xi'an

Same sleeping car as from Nanjing to Luoyang. Clean. Comfortable. Soft pillows, slippers. The car is just for us. Outside: overcast, stormy.

Outside, overcast, dusty, stormy, dry, little vegetation. Hilly steppe. The train goes extremely slowly (it's going uphill).

[We are, with the Agency, passers of walls: we go through the walls of stations, hotels, factories, without any halt, formality, or check.]

4:30 p.m. We haven't travelled 100 kilometres since we left, i.e. in three hours.

On the left of the train, a broad valley with a dried river.

Pale green of wheat.

5:15 p.m. Again the green plain.

Dust outside, until nightfall. Everything is stifled.

8:30 p.m. Since the train is one or two hours late, we are allowed to go to the restaurant car for a while: beer, coffee, bread and jam.

9:30 p.m. Arrival at Xi'an. Two smiling people including one young man who speaks good French. Station-Pagoda.[40]

Station Lounge. Tea. Welcome. Programme.

Hotel of the People. Huge, endless, empty, dimly lit.

The dining room at the end of the world.

We eat alone in a dining room as huge as a ballroom.

Thursday, 25 April
(Xi'an)

7 a.m. Down there, in the alley of a skimpy garden, a man alone, middle-aged, does some gym movements (vaguely like Swedish gymnastics).

And then an awful bellowing starts blaring from the Radio. 'Ah, the neighbours!' a French man would say.

It's a clear grey day, vaguely sunny.

Pagoda of the Great Goose (Tang)
AD 652

A drum is beating in the garden of the Pagoda. Why?

Gardens. Countryside. On the edge of the Garden, irises. Nice weather.

Two small pavilions: one for the bell (morning time), the other for the drum (evening time).

It's calm, deserted.

Seven storeys. 64 metres.

Big French-style garden. Wisteria. Iris. Boxtree.

We go up. I stop at the first level: view over the misty flatness of the countryside. While the others go higher, I go back down by myself. Working-class visitors. Nice weather, breeze.

Departure for the Archaeological Museum. Zhao, in a car, questions me about each of us.

[My phenomenological level = the level of the signifier.
In China, the only signifier = writing (Mao, *da̟ibao*)]

[How intensely they stare at you! Intensity of fascinating, incredible curiosity in the gaze. The reason: this gaze is addressed to you neither as to a person, nor even as to a body insofar as eros, but abstractly and essentially to the *species*: I am dispossessed of my body to the benefit of my germ cells.]

10 a.m. *Prehistoric museum*

Very successful reception lounge.

Luminous, large, fine old paintings. Boy with spotty face and very nice eyes.

Longwinded presentation by a girl with a foxy, pockmarked, clever face. The boy says nothing. (The girl is thirty!)

[Uniformity of clothing means that *in one and the same category* (for example in that of functionaries), this clothing is absolutely uniform and interchangeable.]

Outside, all doors open, the weather is really nice.

Museum loos:

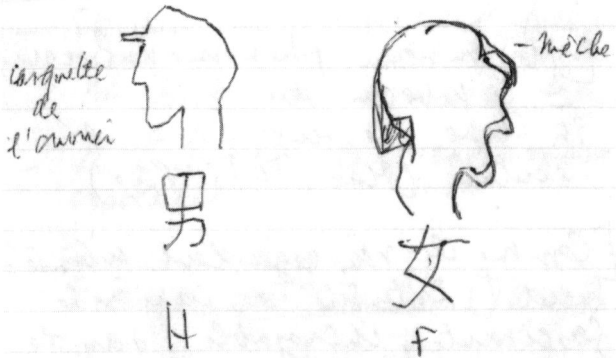

Revolutionary stereotypes ('political practice', the 'workers', 'collectivism') plonked down onto the description of the prehistoric society whose life is reconstructed in the rooms of the Museum.

Boy: gentle face like a girl's (they frequently look like this).

Discussion on the primitive Commune, the clan, matriarchy, etc.

Visit:
[The muddled explanation of this society, given by the clearly incompetent foxy-faced girl, is unfortunately dominated by obvious prejudices: collectivism, platitudinous materialism, absence of symbolism.]

Map with illuminated points (prehistoric sites). If you leave out Tibet, Xi'an is the exact dead centre of China.

The Museum is well designed, clear and didactic. It's busy.
I sit on a bench in the hall: they head off discreetly.
On the far wall a big reconstructed picture; more Soviet-style than realistic; Courbet.

All of this Sino-centric. No idea that there might be societies, villages, etc., like this elsewhere. Blue-rinsed ethnology. No comparative point of view.

A horrible painting, socialist realist: gathering of primitive folk round a fire, a woman with her finger raised, domineering, is speaking; we are told: 'discussion of problems by villagers!'
[Sino- and socialisto-centrism: everything betrays the taste for the cherished commune, for primitive collectivism: *the origin is the model, the guarantor*.]

[Here, the important and sufficient qualification seems to be: high school graduate. Higher education is always ignored: nobody graduates from it. Huge mistrust, no doubt. Everything is staked on the Secondary Schools, then, a few technical institutes, specialized: basically, the same dream as the current regime in France.]

[It's only children who have individualized clothes, with anarchic colours.]

After the visit of the two rooms, didactic and quite empty, elsewhere in the garden, a hall occupied by a huge scale model of a dig (ah, no, it's actually the dig itself).*

Little schoolgirls in khaki jackets, with plaits, satchels and – as ever – *water bottles*. (Soldier, scout.)
None of this seems to go beyond a vulgar negro village.

[1. Discourse of the signifier (writing)
2. Discourse of the signified (Bricks)
3. Interpretation. Struggles. Structures. Processes]

This fake model (since it's real), with its grey, dusty, lunar holes, is deadly dull; peasants, girls, kids, all wander round it with a complete lack of interest.

Sometimes, I enjoy not being interested.

[Level of the signified: in other words: what blocks the place, what bars the signifier. Total eviction of the signifier. In the Museum, difficulty of getting them to say that the painted fish in the prehistoric fishers' Village is a totem.]

Departure from the Museum. Very nice weather. Handing over of insignia (the fish).

[As soon as there is language, there can be no simple materialism. Dogmatic materialism and scotomization of language

---

* recovered from a hall-roof.

go together. Marxist flaw – when Ph. S. maintains a wilfully and aggressively materialist discourse, as soon as he makes of materialism a *direct declarative*, he forgets language and is in short no longer a materialist.]

Afternoon

Strange! We are asked for our passports, 'to be stamped'.

Forty-five minutes by car (it's very hot) to the Peasant Painters. Endless town.
Rare quarrel seen: between our driver and a lorry that wasn't leaving enough room.
Drive past a funeral – body on a peasant wagon shaft.
I am in a really bad mood, because of the passport being taken, the Peasant Painters, etc.

With the Peasant Painters

After an hour crossing pleasant flat countryside – always populated – Village: dense line of inhabitants all along the route: have never been so fêted: Pompidou in Aurillac.[41]

Entry into two or three courtyards. Lounge. Introduced to Comrade-Peasant Painters. Tea.
Overview of the activities of the amateur painters. Welcome (this guy, for the first time, reads welcome notes from a note-book). 40 kilometres away from Xi'an. District: 24 People's Communes, 400,000 men.
Cotton, wheat, rice, maize.
Before Liberation, wretched life under Landowners. After Liberation: become active on the collective path. [One photographs us with decrepit camera.] We have criticized the revisionist Liu Xiaoqi and Lin Biao line. Party's fundamental line

is on the Dazhai model: agricultural output has continually increased.

[On the wall a few paintings by Peasant Painters.]

Production figures [we haven't got to the Painting yet]. Ah yes! here it comes! Liberation on the cultural level. Poor and medium-poor peasants: material and spiritual goods. 1958, Great Leap Forward, a lot of paintings on the walls: the Peasants sang the praises of the Party, of Chairman Mao, and the general line for Socialist Education.

As soon as these paintings appeared, the Party paid close attention; so the District organized training sessions for amateur painters, arts of the Proletariat, for political education.[42] 1958 → 1974: Amateur Painters on the rise: 500 amateur-painters. [Armchairs covered by pink and green terry-towelling.] → Exhibitions [Ceiling: wickerwork and lattice patterns in bamboo].

[Avalanche of bricks. The more cultural, the more bricked-in it is.]

12,000 paintings by amateurs on the history of the commune, etc., 106 shows (collections).

Cultural Revolution: 8,700 paintings to criticize revisionist Liu Xiaoqi and Lin Biao line. Pi-Lin Pi-Kong: the peasant painters have thoroughly studied Marxism-Leninism ('restrain oneself and return to the rites!'). Amateur Painters have thoroughly criticized the will of Heaven and that of the 'Civil servants always intelligent and the masses always stupid'. By practice, they became painters.

Progress in this work, but level of fine arts varies from one brigade to another; some [the lucky ones!] don't have any amateur painters. We are working to reinforce the dictatorship of the Proletariat . . .

Visit to the Exhibition.
[What can one say?!] Pure realism. All in a continuum. Nothing without a content. Even a portrait (a Secretary seated) is reading, studying (he's reading the *Anti-Dühring*,[43] says the author, who's here, and who actually has a handsome slim face).

[They always have bad breath.]
Subjects. Listening to the radio in groups. Reading *dazibao* during irrigation work (current campaign). Group of women hoeing a field, springtime ploughing. (Its intention: to obtain a good harvest, work at every minute.)
[Naïve Sino-centrism: you know, in our part of the world, swallows announce the spring.]
Matter: traditional for painting (watercolour? ink?).
[The ones they show us for a long time are the most polished, the most banal, the least naïve] [for under the daubed surface, a harvest, better, subtle, with a *drawn line* and more naïve arrangement of space. (By the same woman but older)]
In short two types: 1) realist, banal, scene of pregnant instant.[44] (This is the abominable style of posters.) 2) More naïve panoramas, more like Douanier Rousseau, or multiplicative madness. Subjects: tractors entering an orchard. A butcher's reserve (completely crazy!). Education of a young man by an old man in weaving a basket. Cartage of wood. A bright-eyed young girl brings medicinal plants to an old bearded man. Children's ballet. Repairing a telephone wire at night in the mountains.
[There are some that are better than you might think. It's not negative.]
Paintings with drawn outlines, i.e.: drawn and coloured.
[Of course, it's touching, really so.]
Characters always smiling, and ruddy-faced – or pink.
A certain madness of multiplication.

You can see – and this is of value – a lot of paramilitary scenes. A few portraits in crayon: the worst of all. Butte Montmartre. In short, they are excellent draughtsmen. Affinity between Revolution and Drawing (referential illusion).* The surplus is reduced to the rank of *colouring in* (i.e. colour without instinctual drive; colour as plausible).

In the courtyard: nice weather. Two little palm trees.

4:30 p.m. Back to the Lounge.
The place: Huxian.
[Those to whom we were introduced to were in fact cadres, half-cadres of the District, the Commune.]
[I'm not noting all the dialogue where not much that's new; the expected replies arrive without fail.]
5:30 p.m. It goes on! (like the journey).
Goodbye, the posters, maps etc. are put away.
Hilarious: our car moves forward, the gate opens; the dense crowd, all lined up, in a quadrilateral is waiting for us and applauds us.
Back in the car with Julia and the guide who speaks Russian; the countryside and light of the world are beautiful, mild, light green.

[Prohibition *in extremis* of stereotypical language: it gives comfort, security, justification to the subject who speaks, and who in this case ('masses') becomes its subject without usurpation; this language, after all, does not – in this case – take the place of any other, it comes on a non-language, it allows the

---

* and importance (need to analyse this) of the *outline*, the *trait* (of the intelligible).

subject to speak. Quite different is the case of the intellectual who needs to dispossess himself of a previous language.]

[What I am dispossessed of: coffee, salad, flirting.]

Evening: really tired and discouraged. Feeling: I've had it up to here (including the conversations among us). My suit, so longed for, can't be made up here in time and I can't go to the Shop, so all we can do is go for a short walk down the big avenue in front of the hotel: lovely night, slender comma of moon, a lot of people out relaxing, people in the dark alleys doing their gymnastics, a whole little individual life, at night.

Friday, 26 April
(Xi'an)

Again woke up and got up early.
Outside, overcast. In the distance, on a sports ground, young people doing exercises.

[The signifiers: Writing, gymnastics, food, clothes.
(The signifier: basically: everything I like and that alone)]

Breakfast: we draw up the questions to ask the lecturers at the Peking University whom we are – perhaps – going to meet.
We are accompanied, this morning (why?) by the little woman translator who yesterday, at the Peasant Painters show, was there (why?), speaking very good English and Spanish.

Textile factory
(No. 4 in North-West China)

Steps in front of the building (three to greet us, including one woman), lounge with blue curtains, five grey-black portraits.

The tea is served by an old man (obviously, if it's a women's factory).

Welcome in the name of the Revolutionary Committee.

Overview. 1954. Spindles 130,000; 3,240 looms. [On the wall: samples of fabrics.] Equipment conceived and manufactured in China. Cotton thread, every day: 65,000 kg, 340,000 m of cotton fabric per day.

Staff: 6,380. Women: 58%. Line of Chairman Mao and Party leadership → plan established by the state.

Daily life of the workers. Accommodation, Dormitories for the unmarried. Canteens. Medicine: in each workshop + dispensary and near here, hospital. Women given help (child-birth), crèches, kindergartens.

Line of 10th Pi-Lin Pi-Kong Congress: has taken off in our factory; critique of counter-revolutionary crimes, erroneous words of Confucius and Lin Biao.[45] Great progress shown. But still shortfalls: distance from the textile factories of advanced countries [brothers].* So: point out the shortfalls.

Programme for the visit.

Production:

Sorting. Hall. Bales of cotton. It smells like flour, it's hot.

Big green machines that suck in the fluffy cotton spread out in sheets. It emerges much further on in rolls of padded flock.

On the wall poem by Mao in red (with white cotton!).

Great Hall. Weaving, with 1,000 machines, big cords of cotton. All of this clean, humming along, light vapour of cotton, green machines. Red pictures.

Other machines: cords emerge from the threads rolled on bobbins.

The noise gets really loud, we can't hear ourselves any more.

---

* Corrected by Zhao: 'sister enterprises'.

Huge hall with identical machines.

A real hive. The women workers have great manual skill.

The ones sitting down (on small trolleys) are pregnant (Sadeian!).

The threads are wound two and three times.

Fans rotating, gyrating over the threads.

Gluing workshop. It smells of glue, i.e. it smells bad.

Finally the loom Hall: hellish, intolerable noise.

Chiaroscuro of workshop. Checking the rolls of canvas: they pass along a frosted surface illuminated from beneath.

Packaging of the pieces of cloth.

Kindergarten.

Little ballet in the schoolyard. Girls and boys with little white aprons.

Signifier: hands (in the ballets, at the Theatre).

Little dormitories.

The Hispano-British woman translator is speaking more and more with an Oxford accent.

[It's overcast but pleasant.]

Here too the girls are dominant, a length ahead in the games.

Another signifier: kids.

Loads of group games in the yard that fills with sunlight. Games with little red flags.

Visit of families (models).

Inside better than what we've seen. Very clean. Tops hanging up. Radio. Typewriter. Photo of Mao + original (at his desk).

The father and mother + four children. Really kitsch oval plaque. He a machine repairer, she a retired worker.

Tea in the bedroom. At the far end, in the other room, you can see a few books. Mirror. On the wall a cheap print calendar. Wages he: 80 yuans. She: 40 yuans. On the wall: the Nanjing Bridge. All the wages to the mother, who shares it out according to needs.

Accommodation, electricity: 4 yuans per month (two rooms + kitchen).

On the wall, too, an old print, flowers and poem. Little (ugly) lamp on the radio. And Thermos with flowers on, of course!

He: loves the poems, but doesn't understand them, since before the Liberation, was illiterate (laughter). Woman: retirement at fifty. Man: at sixty.

(She somewhat resembles Marguerite Duras.) Looks after the housework and takes part in political activities (reads the papers). (Ch.: she's getting crazier and livelier.)

He: chatty but says nothing, evasive and drowns the concrete details; like a Jesuit, or a Normandy peasant.

On the radio, a small amateur colour photo: the Mother, seated. The old man places his bricks, non-stop.

[Often, in these visits, those accompanying us – from the locality or the Agency – take notes. Perhaps the mania they currently seem to have as a form of study, of social investigation.]

The parents need to tell and teach their children about the miseries of the past.

A concrete example (in the experience of the old man) of the erroneous line of Lin Biao? – Sending educated youngsters into the countryside. [Always the very general Rhetoric of the beginning.] Now, Lin Biao said that this was forced labour. Now he, who had two children in the countryside, has seen that this produced a major change: for instance, beforehand, the children did not know about the fierce struggle between poor peasants and landowners; now they know that the class struggle exists in socialism [exemplary way he sets out the bricks in his reply]. He has been a member of the CP since 1949, she three years later. Since Mao, she's led a happy life. She: takes over from him: Set Theme of the Dreadful past (footbinding, not eating every day)! Her childhood in the old days? Biography, twelve hours per day, was downtrodden, beaten by her boss; hence the family's overflowing love for Chairman Mao.

Brick: 'the revolutionary line drawn by Chairman Mao'.

Iron and steel map, five points (I'll pass over them): two participations, one reform, three Alliances (= Triple Alliance).

Lin Biao: advocated material stimuli and the management of the factory by experts.

[Here confronted face to face by my old fascinating enemy: the Stereotype = the Dragon]

Exit (nice weather). Dense crowd of kids in a compact line, applauding us.

Caricatures of Lin Biao (in the factory garden): he's bald, isn't Chinese, looks like André Gide.

11:50 a.m. End of the Visit.

[Ascending group, movement of the *Marseillaise* by Rude. Let's call this Figure α – derision of the object *a*.][46]

[Skill of an old Party cadre: this means that he is good at *putting together* and *adapting* the bricks – but invents nothing of his raw material.]

[Us: our combinable elements are Words; them, it's the next size up: bricks.]

Afternoon:
Hot Springs of Huaqingshi[47]

Flat green countryside (nice weather), fifty minutes by car. At the foot of a mountain, Red Pagoda, Steps . . .

Very perfumed Lounge, green curtains, shady, big calligraphies. Tea.

Welcome to our French friends. Overview of the springs. 25 kilometres from Xi'an – 2800 BC.
Springs known thanks to Xi'an incident, 1936 (12 December): Japanese imperialism occupied three provinces, eager to push aggression into the rest of China. To resist this aggression vigorously, Chairman Mao and CCP launched major appeal to resistance and solidarity of entire Chinese people; resistance of popular masses; two Kuomintang armies accepted the appeal: resistance and not civil war, and Chiang Kai-shek to renounce civil war; request rejected by Chiang Kai-shek, who had come in person to lead the attack on the red army. But the two armies joined the resistance. Chiang Kai-shek was arrested on 12 December 1936.
After the incident, CCP and Mao decided to resolve this problem by peaceful means. 16 December: Zhou Enlai led a delegation of the CCP to Xi'an. Union against the Japanese.[48]
[There is always the man to bid us Welcome and the man to give us an Overview.]
In praise of the peaceful solution.
Good water: Dermatology, Rheumatisms, Stomach.

Outside. Little pavilion pagodas. Big pond with dirty water. Visitors, little red guards. The green hill over it. Weeping willows. No, the water isn't dirty: dust from the weeping willows.

Little path all round the pond, from pavilion to pavilion. All of this sunlit, mild, floating, charming.

Gardens. Young actors, horribly made-up, waiting for what?

A lot of people, gazing at us, flabbergasted.

In the mountains, we see the pavilion where Chiang Kai-shek was arrested.

They take photos of one another in groups.

The weather is nice, and warm.

Basin under a vault, it's the spring. Climbing white hawthorns.

The House of Chiang Kai-shek.

Under a wide Pagoda awning, big red calligraphy by Mao.

In the garden, the theatre troupe goes to perform before an improvised circle of working-class people. Pi-Lin Pi-Kong play.

We sit on the ground in front.

It's a 'propaganda team'.

[Thick layer of ochre make-up, boys like girls. Eyes vividly painted.]

[I'm right out in the sun, I'm very hot.]

Dance of girls broadly smiling – smiling with all their make-up: these are gatherers who are going to follow the good example of Dazhai.

Flute solo. Active provision of cereals to the state by the peasants.

Joyful song on the steppes. [To be 'in the public eye'.]

Pi-Lin Pi-Kong song. Four girls with stools. One of them

makes a longwinded speech: they are going to produce soles (?) but in their free time they are going to produce criticism (they make the gestures of women sewing soles). One is violently hostile to Lin Biao (all the Pi-Lin Pi-Kong themes pass by). Playlet with musical interludes.

There are some (especially the kids) who have expressions of boundless kindness.

The loos, I ask to go there. Three men are having a shit, collectively. They don't seem in much of a hurry.

We are invited to take a bath. The Emperor's bath had been set apart for me, but it turns out that it's being repaired. A normal bath, a vast tub where there is big jet of hot water at 43°, a bit salty, two little towels, comb. The whole troupe does the same in the neighbouring cabins.

[In short, Mao: a logothete.[49] The logothete replaces the Nomothete.]

Back to the Lounge, Tea, Shade. The others touched by grace, go into raptures over this hot bath.

At the Tumulus of Qin Shi Huang Di, Emperor of the Legalists, dear to Ph. S. (a comparison with Mao). Explanation by the director of the Hot Spring. Flattened hill (this is the tumulus), alone in a huge field of already thick wheat, a high and narrow stele.
The first emperor to have unified China.
Huge countryside, it's 5 p.m., nice weather, the mountain in the distance, distant voices.

This Emperor: representative of the rising class of landowners (247 BC).

The others go up to the top of the mound. I stay by myself and sit on the ground in an orchard, above the wheat field, in front of the vast, floating, green horizon. A few brick buildings in a powdery pink-beige, distant music. A brown beige field, with wide undulating furrows. Trees here and there, in the background. Noise of an invisible motorbike.

Back by car across the lovely countryside with F. W. Fewer people.

[At sixteen, the boys are very attractive. Afterwards not. (Sensual mouths)]

Evening: Ballet *The White-Haired Girl* by troupe from the Province.
The Theatre: a big Pagoda. The plebs. An old Peasant woman with a white handkerchief; the hall isn't full. The people are getting a bit bored.
On purpose, so as to avoid mixing us with them, we are always made to arrive on the dot, the car comes right up to the entrance steps and we hastily, as if furtively, get to (although the entire audience is checking us out) our seats in the front rows.
Big Classical Orchestra, in the pit, with massed choral singers (virile, correct unison, Russian-style).
Overture, some Weber. The rest, Tchaikovsky. F. W. says of the narrative: it's *Jocelyn*;[50] I add: to music by Tchaikovsky, danced like *Giselle*.
Several parts where the girls dance on points, very well, but that's all they do.

I always make sure I'm at the end of the row – so as to sit next to a Chinese person (this man, very much a prole, smiling and distant).

Ballerinas: more gracious, less muscular than the western ones. Since the heroine needs to age, they change dancer, very nimbly, in the middle – with graded wigs.

Interval: we are spirited away, through the side door of the stalls, into a lounge. Tea. Very fine photo of Mao. Calligraphies in Gold. When we go back, half the audience stands up to get a better look at us.

The second part (theme of the victorious Red) is sugary. The positive always comes to a bad end.

NOTEBOOK 3

— Notebook 3 —

Saturday, 27 April
(Xi'an)

Insomnia, Migraine. I get up at six o'clock.
We take our luggage out.

[In short, two problems:
1) Censorship, repression of the signifier. Effacement of the Text to the benefit of Language?
This problem is related to the question: what form of Revolution is thinkable in France, where the way language works is different, specific?
2) Existence, nature, and place of Power. This is a classic problem; it is linked to divergences internal to Marxism: Stalinism/Trotskyism/Leftism.]

Suddenly, it's very dark and overcast, very misty.
The coffee has a totally different taste from coffee, barely even looks it – so light in colour that you often don't know whether it's tea; but with a little milk it (vaguely) creates the impression of a white coffee, and that's enough.
– Our passports? – No problem: this afternoon, or in Beijing!
It's raining, drizzling.

In the Museum of Provincial Life. Umbrellas. Gardens. Pavilions, with porticoes, Pagoda-style.
Two women are waiting for us.
Well, well! No Welcome Lounge!

Museum

Hall: History of the Five Dynasties. Disinfectant. Slave society and Feudal society. Pictures. Dusty bronze objects. This is bound to be really boring. But outside the garden is charming in the light rain, very leafy with steles, units of Pagoda, with red uprights, pine trees, rose bushes – a more French than Japanese place. Shrub of an agave type (there are some of these in Urt).[1]

[Whispers about problems with the plane (wind at Yan'an). How gloomy and oppressive the weather is!]

We slowly and painfully reach the objects in iron.

Can one not speak – applied to History, as our female guide intrepidly does as she comments on the evolution of the display cases – of a dimension of Marxist *fantasy?*]

Two peasants, with padded jackets, completely shaven heads, bags, and peace pipes.
The number of working people who come to Museums, to Shows, is impressive.

[The signifier: rather than censorship, say: the 'silencing'.]
[Imposing silence on.]

Another room (= Tang dynasty) just as long (how promising) – with more 'reconstruction'-type tableaux, Soviet style (the people in them look incredibly unChinese). This is the Historical Tableau style, Laurens.[2]

[Indeed, all public depictions – notices, posters – display Europeanized and virilized morphologies. No relationship with the Chinese *body*.]

The objects become closer, more human, ceramics, silk, coloured statues, Jade, silver plate cups, etc.
Fine fresco with blues and reds, but it's covered by a piece of kitchen plastic.
Break in a rather cold lounge. It's raining. Discussion: since the weather conditions are poor in Yan'an and we risk not being able to land, or in particular leave in time for 1 May, should we leave tomorrow directly for Beijing?
Handing over of insignia: a Tang Horse.

The visit continues. Room of wooden sculptures. Animals (from the Han to the Tang dynasties). At the far end of the room, some Buddhas: at last the body, albeit veiled, appears.

In this room, we speak admiringly of Melville, with Ph. S.

At last the final rooms: Forest of steles. Big collection of calligraphies on stone.
Stele mentioning the entry of the Nestorians (sixth century, beginning of the Tang). Eulogies of emperors, histories, biographies: most of these Confucian.
'You can receive an education from the negative side.'
[In fact, only with the negative can you make art.]

Mao: cursive style, style of Huai Su (a monk).

This museum is boring me to death.

On a big black stele, a big engraved portrait of Confucius, with a beard and pill-shaped hat.

Another stele, a reed whose leaves are Chinese characters.

Last room: Confucian steles. Thirteen classic books. Some squares of characters are surrounded by a line of white chalk: 'restrain oneself and return to the rites'.

[In fact they are continuous *dazibao*.]

On one stele, some trigrams. Initially related to the climate, the weather. But then, the Emperors used them as religious elements to deceive people.

11:30 a.m. Exit from the Museum. It's stopped raining but it's overcast and the wind is cold.

[First Problem: Exhaustion, Rarity of the signifier (related to religious censorship) = this is the level of our journey.

As for the Second Problem (political), complete opacity – and probably one that can be discussed on the basis of documents, without coming here.]

Signifier: don't include clothing: it's here on the side of the signified.

12 noon. Our luggage has been taken back into our rooms. We're not leaving for Yan'an.

There really are too many girls in this country. They're everywhere.

They have apparently asked for our plane tickets for tomorrow, destination Beijing (so Yan'an does seem cancelled) (there's too much wind in Yan'an).

Afternoon

The weather's almost fine.

Administrative Bureau of the Affairs of the 8th Army

Old, clean house. Lounge, Tea. Greeting: she, limp hand. He is former soldier of the 8th army. Welcome. [Very bare lounge in stone. Portrait of Mao and the four others.]

It's the woman with the limp handshake who gives us the Overview.

Organization created by CCP in the region dominated by the Kuomintang. 1936, after Peaceful Solution incident of Xi'an, our party created this Office to organize the working masses in the war of resistance. 1937, cooperation between Kuomintang and CCP → Red Army → 8th Army (September 1937). Recruitment of young patriots and progressives, send them to Yan'an;[3] purchase of provisions for the Front and the hinterland (Yan'an). [Bricks on the struggle.] Then, civil war. Office moved to Yan'an in 1946. Our office struggled for nine years in the region dominated by Kuomintang.

Visit.

Reception room of the Office. Thousands of recruits for Yan'an: 1938: 10,000 people. [Bare little room.] Right now, in the room, newspapers and books. Itinerary Xi'an–Yan'an on the wall: 400 kilometres but a great number of Kuomintang checks: on foot, at the end, sometimes by lorry. In Yan'an, they entered the Technical Institutes. There was also a Women's University.

Another room: the garage. Photo of an old car (for the Party representative) a Ford? For prohibited material.

Another photo: the Office's lorry, with two guys standing on it.

[House with brown woodwork, wickerwork ceilings, inner courtyards with little trees, white walls, black bricks.]

Lounge. Discussion between Officials and Kuomintang.

Photo of Zhou Enlai moustache and little goatee (1935).[4]

Next to it, Zhou Enlai's Bedroom. (His Marxist books.) Portrait of Sun Yat-sen.

Another room: Bureau of the Office and meeting room.

Articles by Mao. Old telephone. Portrait of Mao as young man, uniform jacket and cap with red star.

Basement: in a hole: radio transmitter.

In a yard, small room.

The kitchen (Kuomintang blockade).

In the yard, Well of bitter water.

A lot of small yards, the reason for this being:[5]

Room with big scale model. The present house: in one district = 'Village' of the Genii*[6] (place occupied by the Office during the collaboration with the Kuomintang). The theme is: surveillance of people in the Office by the Kuomintang (secret agents and places for observation).

Etc. (I'm fed up with this.)

Photos: Mao and Zhou Enlai. Mao with long hair.

Several photos of Mao in those days.

[All this of interest because of the Photos.]

Back to the Lounge. Break.

– Questions for the old comrade? – We ask him three: 1) Lin Biao at the time? 'Chairman Mao's closest comrade in arms'? – In fact a commander under Mao's orders; also, he made some military mistakes which Mao corrected. [The old man parries Ph. S.'s attack once and for all with the brick 'Two-Faced'

---

* In fact an area that was then some way away.

and 'Process of Revelation and Process of knowledge'.*] [Fine double brick.]

[It's a thorough-going Scholasticism. Review the bricks of Scholasticism.]

[The old man is particularly bricked-in.]

2) Aid from the Soviets? – Aid from Stalin of course, economic aid. And the spiritual support of the Soviet people.

3) Origin of the funds? They came from Yan'an: in Yan'an, the population played an active part in war and production. The peasants provided cereals and taxes: industry, external trade (with Kuomintang!): salt, medical products. Breeding. Wool.

The separation from Stalin comes when Stalin doesn't break with the Kuomintang (persistent diplomatic relationships), whose line is: active struggle against the CCP and passive resistance to the Japanese. Official break between the Kuomintang and the CCP: 1943. But several *de facto* breaks before.[7]

The Old Man: directed a unit of cadres at the Office.

He fought, was on part of the Long March.

End of the Visit.

Stop-off at the Wall

Xi'an: so that I remember: the town full of cops in the uniforms (white jackets, caps, broad belts) of Tsarist officers. Very Battleship Potemkin.[8]

The Great Wall (a section in the town): no interest except the – tautological** – one of photography! Compact crowd gathers to see us.

---

* These are two different bricks because you can find the one and not the other – but not the other without the first: simple implication.

** or rather: autonymic.[9]

Pagoda of the Little Wild Goose

We stop, but we can see it only from the outside ('you are allowed to photograph it') since the inside 'is being repaired'.
Some pioneers applaud. It's always like this!
The weather's quite fine – a little windy.

4:45 p.m. Return to the hotel. We are informed that we are leaving this evening for Beijing, since tomorrow there are no seats left and on Monday no plane!
5 p.m. We're not sure we're leaving this evening (our luggage has been packed again)! What an imbroglio! Difficult to interpret.
We wait in F. W.'s room.
5:15 p.m. The Beijing plane is cancelled (too windy)! Our luggage is taken back into our rooms! The plane will leave tomorrow, if circumstances permit! Sensation of a real mess. It fills me with anxiety all the same. We all have a drop of alcohol together in my room. We're worried all the same, we wonder what's going on. To console myself, I treat myself to a cigar.

They manipulate bricks (layout, summation) like ideograms.

To the Restaurant! We go there by ourselves, without interpreters. A perfect escape: the chef is waiting for us out in the street and leads us double-quick, with bows and smiles, to a lounge at the rear (rather grim! looks like a converted garage). Delicious meal (big caramelized fish, dish of herbs and meat with a very subtle taste of maize and prawns). We drink a little Maotai.[10]
Leaving the Restaurant: immediately people gather round us,

the chef comes with us and authoritatively keeps the annoying crowd at bay.

Arrival at the Opera. The same scenario as before: the car right up to the very edge of the entrance steps; we dart to our seats, watched by the whole audience.

The most working-class audience we've yet seen. Soldiers, natives with Russian-type sheepskin coats, women with children, old women.

They perform *The Azalea Mountain*: a sort of heroic comic opera with bombastic dialogues, songs, and acrobatic figures. The meaning is glorification of the Party insofar as correct thought as compared with well-intentioned but mistaken outbursts of enthusiasm. The orchestra is traditional.

As ever, they wear over-abundant make-up: the basic hue is a violent purple, leaving the ear white. The Ruddy-faced are the Goodies. The Baddies are paler, in black and in robes (landowners).

Artificial declamation, Japanese-style. The vocal and acrobatic styles (they are amazing acrobats – in the scenes of marching and fighting) are typical of the province (of Shaanxi): this is very attractive. The vocal aspect, raucous, melopoeic, is like Arabic, or flamenco. The fat actor is a virtuoso and wins applause for the intensity, decisiveness, and duration of his melismata (like an Arab woman singer).

Tableau vivant poses – Figure α.[11]

It's another Woman, the Heroine (she's a member of the CCP).

Coded, excessive poses are punctuated by tap dances and drums. (Cf. Baudelaire's 'grandiloquence'.[12])

The actors have castrated voices.

The fat actor throws himself into his role like Greek tragedy.

Another absurd exit: the audience standing, lining up on both sides, applauding us. A crowd around our cars.

Tourism of Kings.

The whole trip: behind the double-glazed window of language and the Agency.

AN ADORABLE PEOPLE.

Sunday, 28 April
(Xi'an–Beijing)

Slept badly despite the sleeping pill Pleynet gave me. Woke very early. It's overcast, still. Are we leaving for Beijing this morning? It's seven o'clock.

The weather lifts, wonderfully clear and mild. At the Airport, empty, but the little plane (twin-engined) is full (Ilyushin 24). (Guys with caps, soldiers.)

8 a.m. We take off. Below, fields, green countryside, square pattern.

Sweets, Cigarettes-Matches, Tea. Below, fields, fields apparently on hillsides.

China: Beige and Pale Green.

It starts to get mountainous, with dried-up rivers that cut through and break up the relief.

9:10 a.m. It goes all flat again. A beige pattern with green areas; the weather is very fine. We drop down towards Taiyuan, stop-off.

We get out of the plane. Sun. The air is extremely pure, as delicious as a cup of tea.

New, very clean little airport. Lounge. Tea.

They all buy little bottles of 'vinegar' (sorghum), for cooking, local speciality.

We set off again. Below, landscape rather jagged as in the paintings. Then it goes completely flat again.
We are served two apples that everyone peels minutely, holding the knife steady and the apple turning.
We land in Beijing at 11:30 a.m.

Beijing

Weather very fine. Hot. Two letters from Mam, but they are old ones.
Minzu Hotel, the room is better and so is the meal, than at our first stay.
General sense of comfort on being back in a capital (although this one seems rather unattractive, with its empty lots, and it still does not give one the impression of a *city*).

All have a coffee in the office of Alain Bouc, correspondent for *Le Monde*. First news from France.

Edgy, though very tired, I can't sleep. Persistent insomnia.
3 p.m. It's very close. We're heading out to do some shopping.

Incident between our driver and a cop at the crossroads. Our driver is violent. Things get heated, another cop turns up.*
Tour of the city, spacious, abundant, lively.
The incident isn't over; the minibus has been parked right in the middle of the avenue for five minutes; a cop in his stand is making a phone call. Our guide is in the stand, trying to

---

* The conflicts here are all definitely all about cars.

negotiate; that's the story. Another five minutes, still no joy. The first cop returns to talk to our driver, who is calmer but indignantly insisting that he was in the right (though he must have gone through a red light). Our guide returns. We head off, without finding out any more.

At the Friendship Shop (for Foreigners): hideous, dismal. A few purchases. A suit? No time because of May Day.
Shopping at the People's Shop: Much better. Very well stocked, abundant, intriguing. Jacket, cap, wickerwork thermos.
Shopping restores me. We are discovering Beijing. At last, a *City*.
The trip assumes a different, more familiar character, more lively, a brighter mood.

Evening: Volley-Ball Match. Girls, China–Iran(?). Huge hall, clean, very well lit (18,000 seats). A lot of empty seats.

[Zhao II has (finally) given us our passports and plane tickets back. Our lucky day.]

Match

Difference between bodies. The Iranian girls: hot-tempered instinctual drive, they snatch their moves ≠ Chinese girls: hit the ball elastically, mathematically. It's immediately obvious that the Iranians are going to lose.
Very modern hall; it doesn't smell of disinfectant.
Many balls in training, like snowballs.
Iranian girls: show-offs, noisy, hysterical. The Chinese girls: poised, icy.
It's very amusing! Chinese girls, every sort of hit: rough,

unexpectedly gentle, etc. The Iranian girls gravely confer; they're brave but have no correct line.

The hall's filled up, very late in the day. People continually walk by in front of us.

The Iranian girls, opulent, broad-hipped, have such breasts!! The Chinese girls are asexual.

They often show their backsides – falling over demonstratively – instead of keeping their balance with a complete pirouette, like the Chinese girls, and they keep yelling.

Next to me, two very fetching boys: 14–15 years old? Their voices are breaking and they are discussing the game in distinguished tones (something British in the Chinese accent, sometimes). They would have delighted a mandarin or landowner.

8:45 p.m. The Chinese girls have of course won the three sets.

Then the boys.

Chinese: the very essence of the body is smooth. Very nice legs.

[Next to me, the two boys hold forth like two small English lords.]

The Iranians are brutes, the Chinese a bit vacant; are they going to lose? Matriarchy yet again! Will force win out over the correct line?

The Chinese have lost the first round; but now, change of Chinese tactics, the situation is turned upside down (9 to 1). No, they flag and fall back again (9–8). Always this matriarchy. [A young French kid who's just been calling for his papa is messing around on the steps. The Chinese smile but don't join in.]

The Chinese are definitely losing.

Monday, 29 April
(Beijing)

Again woke unusually early and migraine. Outside, it's overcast.

Since leaving Paris, as a result of anxiety or curiosity, in short of focus on external things, no movement in my genitals – unless intellectual. But back in the big city, a bit more relaxed, it returns. Dream last night (but Parisian).

7:30 a.m. Under my window balcony, the avenue and a good bit of Beijing, roofs of dusty tile, pinkish brown. The sky is grey but the sun keeps trying to break through.
Breakfast with Alain Bouc.

9 a.m. Departure in minibus for the Great Wall and the Ming tombs. The sun rises, but clouded over. It's not very warm.
All went to Luxingshe to settle money affairs. Pleynet and I pick up 107.45 of the 4,500 F that we had sent from Paris. We are received in a rather gloomy hall. The building smells of disinfectant; not a public office.
I sit at the front of the minibus, next to the driver.
[Bouc did actually ask: given what the trip is costing us, was it all worth it?]
The road out of the suburbs is very long, densely populated. It's stormy.
Flat countryside, green, road still very busy.

[On point I.[13] Censorship of the signifier by the Stalinist *sign*: posters, pictures (apparently the painter has never seen a Chinese man or woman), language.]

Minibus without shock absorbers. Buffeted around like on the high seas.

Signifier: barred by the hideousness of the objects (Friendship Shops).

10:30 a.m. The mountains can now be seen in the distance.
Everyone totally deaf to car horns. What does this mean? Deaf to what?
Ph. S. keeps getting started on France, literature. Endless labelling.
We start moving into the mountains. We follow a gently sloping valley. It's very overcast.
[The only one for whom I'll have needed to show patience will have been Ph. S.]
He abuses the Chinese, who underline each of his repartees with naïve bursts of laughter.
In the distance (we are climbing up in zigzags) we can make out a bit of the Great Wall.
We've seen very few flowers on our trip, very few blossoming fruit trees (unlike in Japan), perhaps because of the very early spring: but what about the flowers?

Great Wall

Arrival at the foot of the Great Wall. Car park. Crowds.

First work on the Wall: during the Warring Kingdoms, 2,500 years ago; at first: walls built up against each other. Unification by Qin Shih Huang Di – 5,000 kilometres. Effective at the time (against horsemen). Current form: Ming.

It's overcast, cold, even icy. People coming and going. The mountain all around is treeless. Down below a few blossoming fruit trees.

Bought and ate an apple. As in all the tourist sites of the world, there is something to eat (a sort of grocer's), drink (tea), a place to piss, there's a letterbox and it's cold.

Go back down into the plain. Turn off for the tombs.

Ming tombs

Thirteen scattered tombs. Flat green countryside. Mountain in the background. Blossoming apple trees.

Picnic in a lounge adjacent to the entrance of the area of the thirteenth tomb. The hotel picnic carton: hard-boiled eggs, cooked meats, duck, cake, apple, beer. Nice weather.
Extremely peaceful character of all these sites.
Peaceful: fresh grass, yellow trees planted in orchards. Incredibly peaceful country. And they were actually always talking about peace (City Names, Heavenly Peace, etc.).

Visit of the Tomb of the thirteenth Emperor, end of sixteenth–beginning of seventeenth century.[14] Pines, Porticoes, Pagoda-kiosks, Pagoda Roofs. Little flights of steps. Cabins selling tea, cards, photos.
Exhibition Cabin for objects found in the tomb.
Headbands of wonderfully green jade. Jade belt.
Big, horrible realistic scale model: oppression, Peasants' Revolt, enforced tenant farming, sale of children.
Crown, belonging to the Empress: blue and stones: kitsch.
Garden, Lilacs, Peonies.
A big modern flight of stairs leads down to the tomb, huge, a real subterranean palace.
Of course, in the tomb, Sovieto-realist pictures showing oppression of peasants.

Outside. Another cabin. Exhibition: Revolt, Uprising of Peasants. Tableau. Movement of ancient peasants. They have the red flag!

Short trip out into the countryside by minibus. Another tomb (the Third Emperor's), this one not excavated.[15] But it's very beautiful, perhaps the most beautiful ensemble we have ever seen: Pagodas, Pines, palms, Small courtyards, porticoes, etc. Blue, red, green.

3 p.m. It's very oppressive.
Wonderful garden: a profusion of flowers, blossoming trees, little yellow kiosks: they are for burning books![16]
Big pagoda hall: empty with huge wooden pillars. Very beautiful. Palace of the Spirit of the dead Emperor. Pillars, brown woodwork, green ceiling, walls with putty placards and a thin turquoise edging.
Chinese visitors: peaceful, 'without attitude'.
All of a sudden in a garden: an awful smell of insecticide of an *unnameable kind.* Or is it a tree, a pepper plant?

Set off again. Stop at an alley of stone animals. I stay in the minibus: the driver (the one who took part in this morning's altercation) smiles at me and does three huge burps, quite innocently, the consequences of his ingesting a (lukewarm) fizzy drink.
Back around half past four. Telephoned Christian Tual. Rest.

Evening: dinner: at the Restaurant with Alain Bouc. Near the Hotel: small working-class restaurant: Huai Yang Restaurant.

A room upstairs, as always. Bouc orders the dishes and the rice wines.

Delicious langoustine fritters, tender, a taste of flour. Mixture of salt and seasonings. (Thyme, perhaps Cinnamon.) Eels from the Yangzi done in garlic. Steamed ravioli, in a big round wooden basket. Several other dishes.

Stiff serviettes.

Steamed bread, fried, crusty: delicious. And a nice cigar.

[Pi-Lin Pi-Kong line: simplistic, leftist no doubt. Movement of rectification, not violent, not attempting at forcing any out. Movement of complexification, thwarting the philosophy of Lin, who aimed to apply Mao's quotations immediately and mechanically.]

At the hotel: Coffee and mineral water.
The discussion continues.

Tuesday, 30 April
(Beijing)

Disturbed night: telegram from Maman. Indigestion.

This morning, as I copy out yesterday's notes, outside, nice haze of good weather.

Foreigners at the Hotel, real pests: two Frenchmen (industry) at our breakfast table. Others cluttering up the small shopping area in the hotel.

The weather is very fine and spring-like.

At the Institute of National Minorities

Isolated buildings in a wonderful garden (the weather is really lovely). Big realistic sign at the entrance: Procession of nationalities.

Flight of steps, several there to greet us, some in suits. A very distinguished old man, brown suit made to measure (and brown cap), very Aragon.

Lounge, etc.

Welcome and Introductions: a few 'representatives of minorities' (professors or students): Korean, Guangxi, North-East China – the old man in brown, professor Li Ou Hai, historian[17] – Mongols, Han,*[18] etc.

[Nice room, peaceful, comfortable. Calligraphy but no portraits. In one corner, an upright piano.]

Outline of the Institute.

Train cadres from the minorities. China: united multinational country. Han nationality + 54 nationalities. Particular attention from the Party and Chairman Mao.

[The Mongol (in green tunic with gold braid): very distinguished and sexy.]

Founded in 1951 in Beijing (but before in Yan'an). 9,000 people trained since its foundation, five departments of sections: 1) Turnover of cadres for retraining (above the People's Commune); studies: a year and a half; draw their salary at the same time. 2) Politics: cadres at the basis and theoretical politics: high school graduates: studies, three years. 3) Languages: training translators in minority languages: five sections: Mongol, Tibet, Uighur, Korean, Kazakh. High school graduates + two years of three great struggles (Class, Production, Science). 4) Art: three specialities: Music, Dance, Painting. Basic courses. Younger students: 12 to 16 years old. Studies: three years. 5) Additional courses: preparatory courses for further education. Studies: two years. Classes in Han language + general knowledge. Wages and Bursaries.

* Hui, Muslims.

Special restaurants for Muslims [in the distance the sound of a flute]. Institute: 1,400 students. 52 nationalities, in the Institute. Students chosen by the masses. Very high level of political awareness. Harmonious solidarity. Currently: revolution in education. Shortcomings.

Programme of the visit.

Visit.

Small exhibition hall. Map of minorities. All minorities = 40 million in 1957. 6% of the total. Five types of writing on the board.

Criterion: each minority in accordance with History, Culture, language, etc.

Display: figurines of fifty-five nationalities. The Han: a worker, cap and monkey wrench.

Big Sovieto-realist tableau. People on a flight of steps with a red carpet, in folk costumes, all smiling.

Display case of local products.

Photos of landscapes.

[Chinese faces: the *decision* in the departure of the eye.]

Costumes and jewellery in glass cases.

Another room: the exploitation of minorities before the Liberation.

Oppression by the Kuomintang. Child with hand cut off by landowner. Photographic evidence. Instruments of punishment. People buried alive in the Lama palaces. Their eyes put out. Hands cut off. Locked up with scorpions. (All this, Tibet as slave-holding region before the Liberation: crimes of the landowners.)

Skulls used as bowls, skins as drums, bones as bugles. Crimes abolished in 1959, crushing of the Dalai Lama's Counter-Revolution.[19]

All the photos are scary. Horseman using a slave's back to mount his horse. Buying and selling of slaves.

Other panels: scenes of revolt. Revolutionary bases.

Third room. Minorities and Marxism.

Garden. Nice weather. Fluff from the trees.

Plane to Lhasa:[20] four hours. Ethnological appeal.

Visit: Translation Class: Uighur. The women, rather gypsy-like, have big combs on their Chinese-style plaits. One has an ear-ring.

A brown-skinned lad, touching, very intent on his work (next to a soldier).

Another class. Translation. Korean. Already quite old. Here: *Dazibao*. Pi-Lin Pi-Kong. Mainly boys.

The Library.

Newspapers in loads of different languages and characters.

Reading tables with white waxcloth covers.

All the students: boarders.

Garden (the weather is so sublime!). *Dazibao* in the scripts of different minorities.

Back to the Lounge. Grouped questions: 1) Liu[21] and Lin lines in the Institute: what problems? 2) Since Confucius was Han, what are the implications for minorities? 3) Non-written literatures? 4) Current tentative progress: details? Religion, materialism? Women? Etc.

1) Reply of the historian of minorities: Before the Cultural Revolution, Liu: counter-revolutionary line. Examples: admission linked mainly to casual examination; old system of education; large masses of the workers were left out; limited

recruitment; owners, aristocrats, lamas, etc. Nowadays, very different: we recruit students Workers Peasants Soldiers. Previously, only experts were trained, and we relied on as yet unreconstructed intellectuals; primacy of professional knowledge: living Buddhas came here to study, as well as reactionary lamas who came to give instruction on the sacraments, etc. Bourgeois intellectuals dominated the Institute. Hence the necessity of a Proletarian Cultural Revolution. After: Mao's instructions on recruitment (Workers, Peasants, Soldiers); reform of studies: before, four or five years; now: three years. Abolition of complicated courses; studies linked to political practice. *Open door* education (i.e. learning in the company of workers and peasants). Link between studies and concrete society. Change in the method of exams: no longer recite mechanically, *open* exam, ability to analyse things. To master knowledge.

Students go back to Tibet and Mongolia and familiarize themselves with the life of the shepherds. We need experts, but *red* experts. – Revisionist line in our Institute? Living example: the exam: previously, consisted in recitals; the teachers considered the students as enemies. This was the exam system copied from the Russians. [From the garden, oddly, there comes the sound of a bugle.] Now: open-theme exam: you can bring your books with you. – Other things copied from the USSR? Yes. The way courses are divided up, since we had called in Soviet experts. [We can hear from the Radio outside the Internationale.] [There are several of them answering the questions in turn.] Soviet revisionist line in the Dance Schools. [The weather, so wonderful, seems, outside, to be clouding over.] Music: manuals copied from the USSR. Only lyric music, in the humanist tradition, could be composed: large-scale forms were preferred, cult of Beethoven and Tchaikovsky; people had no desire to know reality, to compose a revolutionary music: symphony instead of simple revolutionary song.[22] – Dance? Soviet influence: the students seek fame, profit (becoming experts): *Swan Lake*:[23] this isn't the reality of the country: theatres ≠ region of countryside, steppes, mountains, etc. [tired].

[The wind is rising a bit, turning stormy.]

Music: piano: in the past, lessons, basic exercises, Beethoven *Sonatinas*; and afterwards, you couldn't play a revolutionary song, a march. [They each speak in turn, they are very garrulous and hard-line.] Sometimes, of course, basic exercises from abroad, but limited.

12:30 p.m. No time for further questions. Except for one last one, on religion. [F. W. says, about what has just been said: very interesting. I say: bah, predictable.] Religion: 1) freedom to choose religious belief, 2) freedom not to choose, 3) propagate secular theory. Example: Tibet, previously, you did not have the right not to choose belief: one child per family became a lama. Even if you do have the right to choose, we cannot allow people to oppress others with religion. Tibet: before: aristocrats, Dalai Lama, upper class. Tibet: reform of religion. Admittedly, there are temples, but the majority of young people, after studies, lose belief; lamas return to civilian life. [You can't stop them!]

[In my opinion, the session is without interest, since answers are entirely predictable; many bricks, but of a certain level. This represents Beijing pretty well: they are 'well educated'.]

Religion: practised only by older people; not the young.

We leave (it's very late).

Ph.S still giving Religion a bashing. Types of stereotypes: the *severe itch*.

Reminder: the piano teacher: before, people learned 'La Prière d'une Vierge'.[24] Now you can't play this piece unless you first have Prayer. So, from the materialist point of view, reject this piece.

This three-week trip: a good introduction. Intensive Marxist retraining.

[Note: the bricks may be in the translation, since the one person often has a loquacious discourse that makes them laugh, but it's reduced to a brick, a signified, by the time it comes out translated.]

Lunch: Hotel: European-style.

Afternoon
Shopping

Bought prints.
Real little street with booths. Charming.
Second shop. Vases. It's dear and very ugly. All of this served by fragile little old men.
More print shops. Bought brushes of every kind. Bought some nice paper.
At the People's Shop, looked for my jacket – with Julia bought a two-stringed violin.

Dinner: at the restaurant with the cultural attaché Christian Tual, two French students and Françoise Moreux, from Air France.
Another excellent dinner: very dry brochettes (of mutton), Peking duck (with crêpes, young onion stems), caramelized apple fritters.

The students swap stories.

[The indisputable fact: the complete blocking out of information, of all information, from politics to sex. The most incredible thing is that this blocking is *successful*, i.e. nobody, whatever the length and conditions of his or her stay, manages to force it open at any point. Specific dimension, with incalculable consequences, that I can't see very clearly. Any book on China cannot help but be exoscopic. A selective, kaleidoscopic display.]

We go out at about 9 p.m. The buildings are lit up by lines of light-bulbs (for May Day). A lot of people, it's mild, a holiday feel. I'm tired, I go back slowly with Tual, the others carry on to Tiananmen.

Wednesday, 1 May
(Beijing)

Again woke early, got up at 6 o'clock.
This May Day morning looks as if it's going to be splendid: a haze of warm weather over the grey roofs.

No race more hideous than that of the foreigners penned into the hotel: not a single handsome or distinguished subject. Businessmen or philistine tourists. They're particularly arrogant in the morning at breakfast: rested, washed, and guzzling.

[Zhao: Everything in the shops. For this country that was poor fifteen years ago, there's something moving about this. They buy and above all they stuff themselves, they guzzle, it's obvious – they have the finest cuisine in the world at their disposal, and a *structural* abundance of dishes (can be multiplied), opulent flours (wheat, noodles, rice – yesterday I saw a full bag of rice wrapped up and steaming in a goods lift in the elevator. A form of sublimation vis-à-vis the *erasure* of the sexual?)

At Sun Yat-sen Park

We leave the minibus on Tiananmen Square. A lot of people. Enter the Park showing our cards. Crowd. The weather's a little cloudy and warm. Compact crowd.

In the park, shows to be seen on every side. Young girls dancing, as big yellow flowers, as pink workers.

TV sets.

Little stalls of children's games.

Basins, little drinking fountains.

Clothes: a forest of blue and khaki.

Impossible to avoid getting lost.

Sailors. Workers' hands.

Often, here and there, rows of young people stemming the flood of visitors.

Hand-to-hand.

Red flags, lanterns, paper flowers.

Soldiers with loudspeakers directing the crowd.

Red Cross post; they're disguised in white.

We take our seats in an open-air theatre. Huge auditorium, full, little green folding stools. Curtain of roses in front of the stage. Troupe of small children disguised as ducks. Children's orchestra; a little girl sings. Like a star of (Beijing) Opera.

Dance of the little Pine Trees: little girls with a pine tassel and a short green skirt. Dances. Personally, I can't see any difference from *Swan Lake*. The same set of movements, rondes de bras, the same jumps as in classical ballet, soppy smiles.

Kid girls wearing make-up; mortification, mummification.

Several areas blocked off by cordons, attendants.

Peaceful, relaxed crowd. No hysteria, but also no eroticism, and no 'joy'. Nothing odd, nothing surprising, nothing novelistic. A difficult writing, except at certain points, ironic.

Grocery stall (Fruit).

A Red Cross post: an old woman has her blood pressure taken.

Second stop-off. Lakeside theatre. Red Army. A traditional orchestra on the stage, a classical orchestra down below. A woman singer in uniform, very Salvation Army in style, sings a Chinese Opera song with the gestures of the usual code, in spite of her uniform.*

On the lake, small boats decorated with paper garlands.

The singer has finished, she gives a military salute.

Classical orchestra, a tune of the balalaika kind.

Costume ballet (gathering medicinal plants). Chorus in the pit (women soldiers). Still like pantomimes from *Giselle*.

On the side: lovely: lake, grey wall, weeping willows, Pagoda with yellow beige and faded pink roof.

Woman Soldier with really excessive make-up.

We are sitting on folding stools under the pine trees, it is 10:30 a.m., wonderful weather.

Two soldier singers, accompanied by an accordion. Albanian song. One fat and one skinny. Very fine voices, well sung. Trained voices.

The *jeune premier* soldier singer (wearing make-up). No! It's just a flute solo (with accompaniment).

Still too many Foreigners in the audience.

Several games, some of them didactic (music, game of chess) (on a big board).

A soldier as pale as a young girl.

Books.

---

* Women wear skirts only in the army.

Practically nothing to eat or drink.

Hence the (rather childish) *well-behaved* nature of it all.

Fluff from the willows. The water is covered with it.

Goldfish – black – in big tubs.

Exit out onto the Square.

Marx and Engels (hairy): Bouvard and Pécuchet?

At the Workers' Park

Ejusdem farinae.

Paper flowers in real trees.

Stage: a tenor soldier. Fine voice. Accordion. Very Soviet-like.

Another soldier, puny: from him emerges a Russian bass, like Chaliapin. Even the voice is Sovietized!

Break in a room of the Pagoda. Soft drinks. Towel.

I go out for a piss, looking for the toilets. A slatternly girl pops up and waves at me unpleasantly, telling me to turn back.

[Why this *form* of art, among a thousand others, since the criterion, admitted and imposed, is the content? Because this form *comes* from somewhere: Intertext in its immediacy: cadres, *judging* (deciding) or even spontaneously 'inventing': training, either petit-bourgeois or Soviet (it's all the same), which is never *criticized*.]

Outside: red flags in front of the Turquoise of the Pagoda.

Red flags linked by thick wire onto poles in Ming sculpted stone.

Matriarchy of the Army (my poster).

[Greek paradigm: *teleute/askesis*.[25] Here there is absolutely no equalization of the paradigm, evanescence of meaning. Nothing

Dionysian. Where does the orgy go, the *second term*? (in private life).

[Doesn't work through division, splitting – just relocations, subtle slippages.]

Genitalia (the Mother), not phallic. No meaning?

Woman, without transgression, *taken on the spot, like that.*

Afternoon

In the Park of Nationalities

3 p.m. It's still cloudy, very stormy.

[Reminder: yesterday evening: French students telling us that Chinese girls were very jealous. This suddenly appears as highly likely.]

We go to the Park of the Crimson Bamboos. (Display of the Minorities.)

['My outfit, the high point of the trip?'[26] – Oh but yes, to undermine the serious signified of the trip, and add a healthy dose of futility to the good conscience of the political trip.]

Everyone, even workers, takes a one-hour siesta. Work break: 12–2 p.m.

Childish May Day!

Stop off at the Folding Stools. Theatre in the sunshine. Eight cellos (and a piano, in unison, playing something which elsewhere would be Fauré's *Élégie*! Six men, two women in European jackets, without ties.

A costumed Tibetan woman sings with a little traditional orchestra (calico outfit).*

The auditorium is full to bursting. Tightly packed rows all around.

In general, they applaud very little – almost not at all. It's obviously not a habit with them.

Large traditional Chinese orchestra, with conductor on small podium. Nothing but local instruments, two-stringed violins, various kinds of banjos, trumpets . . . and a double bass.

Uighur Dances (Steppe). Choirs. Very Russian tune. Pantomime of a shepherdess learning to read. Here comes the male with the red star. He's bringing her lost lamb back to the girl. The chorus joins in the joy. Very like the Polovtsian Dances.[27]

At the Summer Palace

Countryside, Mountains in the distance.

More festival atmosphere, flags in the complicated enclosure of the Summer Palace.

Little pink and yellow girls. At least these ones give me a smile!

Chorus of little boys wearing make-up.

Compact rows, faces stretching away forever. Jostling. Kindness.

Great Lake, surrounded by Pagoda Palaces: boats disguised as ducks, big red balloons over the water.

Charming little stone terrace over the lake.

– It's overrun. Gallery-path, covered: winding walk.

* She sings: 'the freed slaves enter University'.

Break for soft drinks in a delightful courtyard. Smiling welcome from waiters in white jackets, many of them. Fine afternoon. Curving roofs, grey, pagoda-red, lattice pattern, green panelling, etc. It's five o'clock.
Peaceful, peaceful . . .

Towards the stone boat. A boat filled with officials sails past; the political bigwigs are all sitting under the boat's veranda, taking tea without any communication with the crowd running avidly along the shore to follow and see the boat. Avidity.

Opera Theatre. Another girl dominating the treacherous boy (all in black) – with their hair in little bunches, phallus-like.

Around 5:30 p.m., the crowd peacefully heads to the way out of the Summer Palace, in the midst of an ever-louder Internationale.
Back in the coach: huge crowd leaving, seen from behind.

May Day between the childlike and the childish. But too many children, an indigestion of children, a civilization of infantilized children showing off in front of passive crowds of rather dazed adults.

Evening

[Infantilized adults.]
[The adultified children infantilize the adults.
The children as *spectacle* for the adults.]

Sports display

In the fine big hall where we watched the Volley-Ball. A lot of people but many foreigners, alas. We wait for half an hour (until eight o'clock), it is intensely lit up; applause; who is presiding?

Dance hall piano. Troupe of girls in bathing costumes, about thirteen years old; a sort of flyover; actually, a lot of them botch their entries. They are slim, so slim, long bare thighs.

A march on the piano. The males march in, white tracksuits, sleeveless vests. They don't land well. All this nice and elegant: neither American nor Russian, for once! They march off.

Gymnastics on the ground: sweet little girl on the green carpet: acrobatics, grand écart, double leap, etc. The sweetie runs off.

Thirteen-year-old boy in white, the same acrobatics. Sixteen-year-old girl, etc. All this to piano accompaniment. Half gymnastics, half dance. Fifteen-year-old boy, etc.

Boys on the vaulting horse. (These are students from the Institute for Sports.) This exercise is really boring.

[They never seem to get the jitters, nowhere.]

Hyper-western ditties.

All this is boring, brave, and inauthentic.

Boys-Young Men: the rings. The commentary insists on how young they are: performance-education.

They often botch it (almost always), and above all: so very conventional: no poetry.

The sweet little girl in red, twelve years old, keeps coming back for her dances – little acrobatic turns on the ground. She's a bloody bore!

[A May Day that's disappointing, dull, not at all heroic or revolutionary, terribly prosaic.]

Parallel bars.

Etc.: completely meaningless – and botched.

Second part: traditional (Wushu).*[28] Alas, it looks like something in the Ballet line, seen endlessly during the day.
[A country where there's nothing Political that's Text, i.e. in the final analysis a signifier – in any case not Art!]
No, it's a bit better than the Ballets: more acrobatic.
One boy alone, in pale green: combat gymnastics. Another – a kid – with a sabre. Girl in white with a lance. [Amazon]
[They're not naked any more, light, wide trousers in white; blue-green blouses, gilded decorations.]
It's very repetitive and boring.
They fight in twos: very quick and coming to a sharp halt.
Nimble scene: a little sweetie of a girl and two little boys; each with a lance: the girl attacks the two boys suddenly.

[I had initially classified the children among the few signifiers, but they now strike me as a real bore.]

[Can one claim to be developing political awareness without developing intelligence (reflection) as well? Can one sharpen one's wits politically and infantilize the rest?
This May Day paradoxically gives me the terrifying image of a humanity engaged in a political struggle to the death in order to . . . infantilize itself. Could the child be the future of the man?]

10:30 a.m. We emerge from this interminable session feeling exhausted and depressed.

Thursday, 2 May
(Beijing)

7 a.m. The weather is fine, cloudy, outside.

---

* Wu: army = military art.

I have breakfast before having a wash. While waiting for the Barber and the bank, a walk outside: nice weather, spring-like, wonderful. The drivers of the lines of cars are cleaning their vehicles with long feather dusters: a little bucket in front of each car.

At the Barber's on the tenth floor. All done by electric clippers. Shampoo: a few massages.

9 a.m. *Information session with Luxingshe representatives*

In the lounge on our floor, in the hotel.

There are three of them, speaking French (plus Zhao I): an older one who speaks very well (from Shanghai).

Welcomed by the eldest: to learn from us about France.

I. Presidential elections?[29]

Mitterrand and the bourgeoisie?

Unfavourable economic situation?

Purchasing power of the workers?

Petite bourgeoisie?

Contradiction between Socialists and Communists?

How do Chinese comrades see the USSR developing? – Refuse to reply, we don't know, we are in China, etc.

Prospects for the Protest movement after the elections?

II. Working-class movement in France? (i.e. leftism).

Leftists' movements?

Trotskyism? (this interests them). [The only point on which they make a definite statement: not many Trotskyists, but they sabotage the Revolution.]

Lin Biao? – No reactions. (They don't like it to be said that people in France don't understand the Pi-Lin Pi-Kong campaign.)

III. Crisis within the French CP?

[11 a.m. Outside, it's cloudy.]

The current Socialist Party and the old SFIO?[30]
The Army?
[All the questions – infrequent, factual – are not very committed. The overall meaning of the session is implicit.]
Women, Abortion?

Was it a courtesy session? It almost seemed like one. Were they really from the Agency?
Resurgence of egocentrism in the political: Ph. S. sees the CP in relation to him, China in relation to itself, etc.

Lunch (disagreeable) with the Mavrakis and the Luccionis, residents here. We travel by taxi to a very commercial and very populous district, to the *Peking Duck*; but it's inevitably a matter of eating 'like the people' (i.e. revolutionary style), in other words in the same room as the Chinese and not that of the foreigners. Negotiations, we wait while walking up and down in Indian file in the busy street. In the end it's not possible; so we go up into a big dining room where there's an excellent meal (duck liver, Peking duck with sesame pancakes); the Militant's tedious discourse.
Mavrakis informs us, in triumphalist tones, and altogether to the glory of China, that this evening there are couples of lovers in the Bamboo Park! You can see, he says, that there's no repression here!
Every French person, here, has his own little idea about China and speaks of this idea alone, absolutely deaf to the other!
Back in taxi (ouch!), we are all exasperated. It's hot and sticky.

Afternoon

At the Temple of Heaven

In a big park, full of people, streamers, crowds: it's still a holiday.

Different buildings, quite flashy: remarkable for the blue-beige marquetry of their roofs.

]pp[It's terribly hot, oppressive, bright afternoon sunshine. The coach, waiting for the driver, is surrounded by a crowd of open-mouthed children. Civilians, with a serious and distant demeanour, gently try to shoo them away, simultaneously out of a sense of propriety and distance towards the foreigners.

Shopping

Friendship Shop. Ordered a made-to-measure suit, Christian Tual can bring it back for me. Wonderful old-timer who measures me up.

Bought cups with lids.

In a Chinese Chemist's shop: Julia inquires about contraceptives.

In the hotel: saw two French students, to whom I handed over the receipt for the costume, for Tual (for 23 May).

With Bouc, at the Sichuan Restaurant. Charming courtyards, almost rural. Little dining room on the ground floor, overlooking a simple yard (old aristocrat's house). Pretty chinaware.

Very lavish meal, exquisite, spicy, with several dishes: at the end, wonderful warm puree of nuts.

We slowly walk back through the narrow streets. This makes it all different; it's the first time we can see the streets independently. The moon, the sometimes dark street, trees, it's warm, people coming and going, little houses, open to the street, residents bringing out their (dry) rubbish: at last, a certain eroticism possible (that of the warm night).

Friday, 3 May
BEIJING

[Note from yesterday: Luccioni, speech at lunch: he makes an intent and constant effort to speak about China from the point of view of China; a gaze coming from the inside – all his efforts to speak *from the inside*: clothes, rejection of the foreign restaurant, bus and not taxi, Chinese 'comrades', etc. At the other end of the spectrum, Tual and the students continue to see China *from the point of view* of the West. These two gazes are, for me, wrong. The right gaze is *a sideways gaze*.]

6 a.m. Outside, grey mist. [I now have a neurotic fear that some accident of the weather will stop the plane from taking off tomorrow.]

To visit the University, a big deal, we have three extra interpreters! So there are five of them altogether: five on five, that's the real principle.

Trips in the minibus are irritating because they are an opportunity for Sollersian orations aimed at the interpreters.

At the entrance to the University, we are stopped, they need to telephone.

Peking University

In a wonderful, deserted campus: pavilions, gardens. Welcomed by three and four characters including a woman (Revolutionary Committee and teachers and students).

Rather old room in a pavilion-pagoda. Calligraphy.

Welcome. Introduction. The lecturer in literature. Dean of materialist and dialectical philosophy + Professor of literature + philosophy student + cadre from Bureau of Administrative Affairs + *id*.

Programme.

Overview University: 1898. Three disciplines: human sciences + nature + modern languages. 2,300 teachers. Students: recruitment not explained, figures still limited: those for 1974 have still not entered.

After the Liberation: major development. Before the Cultural Revolution because of the Liu line, it was impossible to apply revolutionary Mao line in education. Liu copied the Soviet system of education = old system: University cut off from Workers-Peasants-Soldiers and concrete social reality; primacy of professional knowledge, quest for fame and individual profit. This erroneous line could only serve to educate aristocrats from the bourgeoisie [outside, pine branches. Shade inside the lounge]. In 1966, Proletarian Cultural Revolution → August 1968, representatives of Workers and Soldiers entered the University. Since, Revolution in education.

Following the teachings of Chairman Mao (education must serve proletarian politics, linked to production) → radical change. Change:

– Admission, recruitment of students. Previously, recruitment of high school graduates and exams. Now, graduates go into the factories and the countryside. At the University Workers

Peasants Soldiers with practical experience. The candidates express their desires, discussion by the masses, approval of the official from the Prefecture (above the district, below the province), ratification by the University. So: young people with socialist political awareness + practical experience + general knowledge. Mainly: political criteria (study of Marx, Lenin, Mao + devotion to the People). You first need two years of practical work. [Very long blue table, windows with decorative woodwork.] At the University: cultural knowledge + industry + agronomy + military art + ideological critique of bourgeoisie and revisionism. The State subsidizes everything or wages. [Continual tea.]

– Change in structure of Education. University: open door (class struggle, production, science).

What a student earns (food + pocket money): 15 yuans (food) + 4.5 (pocket money) = 19.5 per month. [A packet of cheap cigarettes: 0.40.] [A meal in a cheap restaurant. Sichuan noodles: 9 fens.]

Links with factories outside the University: students go there periodically. Example: electricity: workshop where electronic devices are manufactured. Appropriate computers, mastered by the students. Before: just book learning. Human sciences: the whole of society is their factory: connection between Marxist-Leninist theory and struggle: a third of total time within society. During these last three years, students of Human Sciences → 165 factories, communes, magazines, editions. Social surveys. Human sciences = Chinese language, history, philosophy, economy, international politics, law, libraries.

Example: society = factory: Lenin is studied in classes [the rest of the demonstration is lost in translation; the pattern is: in going to the factories,[31] to find in them the dossiers of imperialism in the old society: history of the enterprises]. Thus, the students know the nature of social-imperialism; the action of the two super-powers pillaging their way across the world. Articles by the students and professors: of a high level.

Another example: literature: before, they did not educate creators; they simply taught the theory and history of literature. But recently, the students can produce essays, poems, novels, reportage, really reflecting the concrete struggle of the WPS. They joyfully say that they can learn what people could not learn in the past.

Example: Philosophy: twenty students in two months could criticize and explain the conversations between Confucius and his disciples.

The students dare to do what the ancestors did not dare. They have translated them from the classical into the modern language, while criticizing them. Professor Feng Youlan, at the age of eighty, has researched the ancient history of China.

– Reform of the content and method of Education. Old manuals poisoned the students; overburdened and confused, with idealist residues (Manual = printed book and the course).

Republication of the Manuals: 1) Dialectical materialism = centre, 2) Linking theory and reality, 3) Liquidating everything confusing and burdensome: simplification: 'little and better', less and better.

800 teachers → 500 manuals.

Method: liquidated cramming. Now: method of *suggestion*, and discussion to enable the students to think for themselves. From 1970, 5,600 students WPS. Already: 2,300 graduates. And yet the period for study has been reduced: now: three years. Also, ability of new students to analyse and solve: higher than in the past. But still an entirely new thing: nevertheles correct and lively guidance.

Many problems, contradictions. Balance sheet necessary. We

await your suggestions and remarks to improve our work (10:30 a.m.).

Some questions

The presenter: Niy Mang Choung: head of Revolutionary Committee of Peking University, specialist in Russian, Bureau of Administrative Affairs, Chairman of the Department of Russia (Beijing Daxue, Peking University).

Most students return to where they were sent from. A hundred students remain at the University (research where it is needed). The student formulates his desire for discipline but in accordance with the need of the State, or of the Commune. Desire expressed in three classes, for example: 1) Maths, 2) Physics, 3), etc.

Human sciences: International Politics, archaeology: they learn modern languages. First language: English, then Russian, French, Japanese, etc.

Three departments of modern languages: 1) western, 2) eastern, 3) Russian.

– Essays, poems, novels, etc. by the students? Published articles (once they have matured with the professors): newspapers, periodicals. News, more than novels, reportage ('the Revolution of Spring and Autumn').

– Difference between wages and bursary (around 20 yuans)? No contradiction, since sometimes, the young, volunteering to abolish pocket expenses, are helped by families; the others, often, kept by families.

– Only unmarried, here. Age? Entry: about 20 years. The eldest (rare cases): 27, 28, 31 years. Women: ⅓.

– All boarders.

Professors: around the University, University accommodation (University halls of residence). Some live with the students.

11 a.m. | Basic questions | (sent in advance).

[A girl with plaits and a white jacket keeps the tea and cigarettes going.] [It's calm, old-fashioned, an aristocratic place. Calm and art of living of a campus in the American South.]

Break: they have recorded the questions – asked again by Ph. S. They are going to reply – doubtless each one depending on the case and the example.

[On the wall: two ancient scrolls: horses.]

Replies

– Personal point of view of one. – Pi-Lin Pi-Kong, an *extension* of the Cultural Revolution?

– The Cultural Revolution has reinforced the proletarian dictatorship and political awareness, class struggle. We have liquidated two revisionisms: Liu and Lin. Achievement of the Cultural Revolution is important; but we know that the struggle continues afterwards. Thus, problem of yes or no to the Cultural Revolution. Lin's opportunism actively slandered the Proletarian Cultural Revolution. To counter the right-wing tendency to go back to the past, it is necessary[32] to evaluate the Proletarian Cultural Revolution positively.

– This right-wing tendency, when?

– Difficult to answer, since process of struggle. (Before/ Afterwards = 9th Congress.[33]) Lin, sometimes, carried out direct attack, sometimes denied the new things that appeared at the Cultural Revolution. Same tendency as Confucius. Lin shouted a few slogans for the Cultural Revolution but this was not the essence of his line; Lin's overwhelming hatred for these new things; criticized the settling of young educated people in the countryside. Same line as Confucius: restoration, regression. To your face sings your praises, the little book in his hand, but seeks to stab you in the back. The proletariat is strong, so people take on its mask.

[There is no escaping from bricks.] So Pi-Lin Pi-Kong: close link with the Proletarian Cultural Revolution. So, it is indeed an extension.

– Another reply (Zhao, philosophy prof?): on the revisionist line and relation revisionism/dogmatism. Lin line: revisionist line 'to restrain oneself and return to the rites'. This means: to restore capitalism [it's starting off with a fine display of bricks]: back to restoration. How is this shown? Lin took measures to usurp the power of the Party and the State: advocated Presidency (proper name).

[All this: obvious that the purest production of the regime is a formidable *Rhetoric*: art of persuading, of convincing, i.e. leaving language without gaps, without second thoughts.]

Lin has undertaken counter-revolutionary coup d'état. Betraying the dictatorship of the Proletariat = key point of all opportunists. Hence Pi-Lin Pi-Kong: struggle against revisionism.

And also: struggle against revisionism in the superstructure. Lin wanted to liberate politically the bad elements, the right-wingers, the opportunists, the landowners, etc. On the international level: asked for the support of social-imperialism and imperialism: nuclear umbrella of the USSR. So we say of him: super international spy. Seeing his foundations, we can say that he represents all opportunists. On the theoretical foundations, he preached the theory of genius (idealist apriorism): knowledge and competence are supposed to be (innate) gifts from heaven. [This is the perfect lesson, very complete and clear]; but historically, it's an idealist conception: all this is to prepare public opinion for restoration. Theory of the genius of the leaders: in fact to undermine the prestige of officials. He considered proletarian officials as supermen: separated the leaders from reality, from the masses, from the proletarian class. He

(Lin, that is) considers the officials as kings, as feudal emperors. In appearance, he elevated their positions, but in fact he denigrated their image. Cf. the way in which Stalin criticized the Trotskyists brigands, who sang the praises of Lenin as a genius; but it's not sincere, intriguing against Lenin. [Don't upset the lesson's plan: 'I'll come back to this later.']

Carried the red flag to oppose the red flag. Considered himself to be a genius, a leader – and the son as a super-genius! (the son was 23, is dead, 'departed to meet Confucius', studies at the Peking University, but he was a fool! Lin Liguo).

To realize his bad intentions, reactionary words.

[They can never reply to factual, historical questions. The discourse is always *general*: a sort of monstrous ventriloquism.]

12 noon. Two girls brings saucers. We're going to have a snack. [Admittedly, we're not in the universe of historical science! The way historians go out of their way to furnish proof of an intention!]

[The girls bring plates of little sandwiches and cakes.]

[We are always raising the question of the *document*; but there's never any reply; we're not in the historical universe, rather, says F. W., in a Lacanian universe!] [We are referred to *types of discourse*, that of Zhou Enlai for example.]

Break: we have a bite to eat. Beer.

Why the *Gotha Programme*? Because it's a glorious work, and against opportunism: don't make compromises over principles. Sharp sword against revisionism, and: period of transition from Socialism to Communism (Dictatorship of the Proletariat).

The meaning of Pi-Lin Pi-Kong: to insist on the dictatorship of the Proletariat: continuation of the Revolution under

Proletarian dictatorship. Defence of violent Revolution against Lassalle's thesis. So a struggle against Revisionism.

Discussion during the break: on Work, the beginning of the *Gotha*. The professor of philosophy defends his ideas better.

[Two pots of geraniums, symmetrical, under Mao's mural calligraphy.]

Primacy of class struggle over 'development of production'.

[Our supplement of interpreters has remained completely silent, taking notes.]

It's 12:30 p.m. We've been at this table since 9:30 a.m.

[It's a discussion between the philosophy professor and Ph. S., who greatly enjoys this duet: he's talking! he's the boss!]

Philosophy Professor: excellent knowledge of Marxism, an answer to everything straight from the Corpus, from the Vulgate: an excellent priest. Worthy to teach the catechism!

[Bourgeois universe: positivism, historical Science, world of proof, of the experimental, etc. ≠ Marxism: discursive and argumentative phantasmagoria,* without 'proofs'; return of Mythology? return of Discourse?]

[But perhaps in the eighteenth century, in the period of the bourgeoisie's rise, the rising discourse might have struck me as equally catechistic.]

[It will be necessary to distinguish what I have learned *on the first level* and *on the second level*. (It's rather like 'the sideways gaze'.[34])]

---

* with its big negative Phantom Words: the Real, Political Practice, etc. Great Verbal Beings.

[Excellent little sandwiches: a sort of wholemeal bread with ham and pork.]

[You can hardly get them to admit to the least anti-Stalinism; they always defend Stalin – it's Khrushchev who is attacked] – Stalin: possible mistakes, but Khrushchev and Brezhnev: traitors. You can't compare a comrade who made mistakes with traitors (to the Proletariat).

[We would have:
I Level of the Signifier
II Level of the Signified (discourses produced)
III Level of the Text making and unmaking itself (real politics, struggle between different lines, etc.)]

[I let the discussion pursue its course, although it's interesting, especially on the causes of the appearance of revisionism in the USSR.]

[In front of me behind the decorated windows, such a French landscape, almost like the South-West: pines, plane trees.]

Theses on the mistakes made at the end of Stalin's life: contradiction between theory and practice: he practised class struggle but said theoretically that it no longer existed. He was a very great revolutionary, capable of correcting his mistakes. But didn't have any experience, since the only socialist country. Responsibility for revisionism cannot be laid at the door of Comrade Stalin.

Discussion interrupted without beating about the bush, time for a walk, as things were getting awkward.

Walk:

Walk in a group in the solitary park. Lake. Radar in front of Pagoda. Tomb of the Ashes (part of them) of Edgar Snow, 'an American friend of the Chinese people, 1905–72').[35]

This University, from which the Cultural Revolution emerged – is completely empty, peaceful – and has the wisest discourse imaginable.

Collective photo.

The Library: empty, it smells of camphor. Portraits of the four and of Mao. Overview given by the leader in a cap. [It's as if the University has been completely emptied, exhausted in our honour.] It's dark and cold. A rather modest place.

The librarian's bricks: inheriting the cultural patrimony while criticizing it (this is said in front of ancient manuscripts displayed in glass cases).

It's very clean, it smells of camphor and Indian perfume, a Chinese Chemist's.

Corner for French literature: Molière, La Bruyère, Fénelon, Doumic! Lanson! and even me in the Picon! but it's still uncut![36]

The weather's very fine, very calm. At 2 p.m. bicycles appear. Everything is very scattered in the park. Where are the collective activities, the *da$_{\gamma}$ibao*?

2 p.m. Back to the Lounge. After the break, the professor seems to have recharged his batteries and a good store of bricks; he launches into an attack on the evil influence of two revisionist lines.

[Every Marxist assertion is 'unproven'; or rather, Marxist discourse is purely assertive. And this enables all the fractionist

languages, within Marxism, to argue with one another by uttering homogeneous assertions: it's the same difference.]
The professor purely and simply repeats himself: idealism of the theory of genius, 'heroes create history', etc.
It's the pure world of the Catechism.]
The unhappy, and naïve, man does not suspect that we have heard his speech in its entirety, ten times already. Or is this of no importance to him? Change of value: originality is no longer a value, repetition is not a drawback.
The professor carries on with the list of Lin's crimes (all of them abstract), and bricks.

[We would have: the Discourse (awful) ≠ the Real (the satisfaction of needs), glorious.]

[In short, it's the virgins who wear plaits.]

[I doze off as at a lecture, or at a sermon which resumes its strophes after each translation.]

[A Discourse against a Need? This is the problematic equation.]

[Everyone agrees repeatedly, at the expense of revisionism – forgetting the awkward fact of Stalin, the source of disagreement.]

Lin Biao, Bushido, and Hitler. Wanted a feudal fascism (≠ Mao: it's the Party which runs the Army).
Confucius and the family? – His influence in every area, since it's been spread by all successive dominators. Confucian ethics: major influence on family: fixed in the shape of four powers:

political, classic, religious, marital – four chains of the Chinese people. The husband's power: he was very fierce: wife subjected successively to the Father, to the Husband, to the Son. These harmful influences have greatly lessened and still need to be completely liquidated. With Confucius, obedience cultivated to the advantage of slave society. – And now: authority and obedience of one class? – For the Proletariat, Revolution: the strongest authority: centralism + centralism = authority. – The place of 'against the tide'? – Those who go against the mistaken tide of the bourgeoisie do so merely to create and reinforce the authority of the Proletariat.

[Outside, the University is unchangingly empty.]

'It is right to rebel against reaction' – to establish, through the struggle, the authority of the Proletariat. The Cultural Revolution? Always under the leadership of the Party, with Chairman Mao at its head.

With regard to Confucius: nowadays, is the very principle of the family being questioned? – The bourgeoisie had denigrated Communism, saying that it sought to weaken the family. To this Marx replied by saying that in Communist society the family would have vanished. But the family: historical reality, very different from one period to the next: example: Patriarchy = private property; family = unit of production. Bourgeois family = relationship of money. So the character of the Family must change; but it will never disappear: it always remains as a human blood tie; this tie must develop and can never retreat; ≠ capitalist country, where young people dream of destroying the family with disordered sexual relations: this is a return to primitive society.

[Importance of the theme: 'don't retreat' = Form! the content is of little importance!]

Further questions: criticism of the Chinese cultural tradition as a whole? Positive aspects of intellectual work in the western world? Literature and Linguistics?

Replies: Classical Chinese literature: attempt to liquidate the influence of Confucianism + attempt to study the tradition of the Legalist School. [Perhaps this pile of bricks because they are being listened to, not by us, but by themselves.] Progress was always associated with Legalism. [The *renewed* blandness of the tea is homologous with the repeated blandness of the speeches.] Currently, the main problem is Confucianism/ Legalism [nobody bothers about Daoism, Buddhism, etc.] [The woman too, who has a pretty accent, starts to pile up her bricks.] Principle: inherit, in a critical manner: what is ancient must serve the present. All research: through Pi-Lin Pi-Kong + Theoretical problem: how to create images of heroes, how can literature serve the WPS?
– Lukács? Revisionist.
– Linguistics? – Department of the Han language. 1) Modern language, 2) Classical language, 3) Theory and history of the language. Guidance: criticize the bourgeois and revisionist theory of linguistics in the light of Marxism. Vulgarization of the spoken language of Beijing: reform, simplification of characters. Follow the path of latinization, since in spite of the huge contribution made by characters to Chinese civilization, there are drawbacks. Research into the numerous dialects to discover common rules shared by dialect and Beijingese: speak them at the same time. Later, it will be possible – after the general spread of the spoken language – to romanize the characters, although the two tasks are being carried out at the same time. [The strangest thing of all isn't China but Marxism taken to a radical degree.]

— Opinions of western linguists re. the Chinese language: they are not objective, don't correspond to the reality of the Chinese language. Link Chinese reality to this research. How to use this Han language with simplicity.

[This University: super-orthodox, super-radical, super-catechistic, and thus, in practice: *avant-garde* — but not in our sense of the word!]

We are leading the struggle against the bourgeois linguists of Western Europe and the revisionists. Western and reviso theory[37] = inadequacies; for this theory: based on Indo-European, thus incomplete character of this theory, since they have not included the great and splendid Chinese language into their system. So our research: great significance, extending linguistic theory and correcting failings. Conforming to the appropriate character of every language.

As for the linguistic synthesis, all languages need to be taken into account. France, a country with a linguistic tradition: in future, we hope for a reciprocal linguistic contribution.

Questions:

— Our students know about USA research on Chinese language; a group of Chinese has been sent to USA, various Universities and linguists. — Problem: linguistics in the service of Politics? Inadequacies of Europeans? It would take too long to reply.

— How can we know about this research by Chinese into the Chinese language? Since the Cultural Revolution, haven't had time to publish reviews. This will depend on the concrete circumstances. And even here, class struggle between the two lines.

[Absolute political totalitarianism.]
[Political radicalism.]

[Personally, I won't be able to live in this radicalism, in this fanatical monologism, in this obsessive, monomaniac discourse] [in this *fabric*, this text without a gap.] [Chauvinism, Sino-centrism.]

We think that the Chinese language is very precise; that one can express what one thinks very precisely.

Thanks from Ph. S. and reply by Professor of Philosophy: very deep, very wide-ranging talk with the *Tel Quel* group. We don't feel tired, we feel joyful. Our Talk will facilitate the French people's understanding of the Chinese people.

It's 4:40 p.m.
Outside, fine weather, calm, bamboos, yellow flowers, a basin in the small yard.
We walk past a short column of students.

Hotel: Maotai all together in one of the rooms.

Last meal – at the invitation of Luxingshe

Shantung Restaurant. Rather a luxurious dining room, 1925 staircase. Tea, warm perfumed towels. Welcomed by the Big Boss of Luxingshe (longwinded, never-ending speech on the 'shortcomings').
Obvious the division of the three costumes of the Luxingshe agents: the Big Boss, dark suit, very clean; the deputy who organized our trip, quite a slender young man, beige cloth jacket; our interpreters in shabby jackets or little cotton suits.
The Big Boss makes a political speech with facts and figures.
Dish: sheep's stomach, etc. Very nice.
Walk around the hotel before packing bags.

Saturday, 4 May
(Beijing)

Woke at 5 a.m. for the departure. Feeling on edge. Outside, very overcast, last Pagoda roofs, last car horns.

7 a.m. We set off in the minibus. Avenues full of blue workers on bicycles. On Tiananmen Square, red guards in blue and white doing a sort of exercise in rows. A column of young people crosses the avenue.

Formalities: too many! a whole oppressive circuit.
Lavish breakfast at the airport Restaurant.
A lot of people, a lot of Chinese in groups, in lines, in uniform: in their dark uniform jackets, with closed collars, they look like real Jesuits.

On the plane: outside the weather is fine and spring-like (during the trip to the airport, we could see mountains in the distance).
9:05 a.m. We start taxiing (the plane is full to bursting: Alsatians, Blacks, Chinese, etc.).
No sooner are we on the plane than the usual crap from Air France (i.e. France): the hostess looks sour: this baggage should have gone into the hold!
9:10 a.m. We take off.

PHEW!

Vulgarity of the hostess who, handing out newspapers, says in front of us: 'I don't believe it, *they*'re going to fight!'

On the Plane

Some prices for merchandise:

A pound		
	Rice	0.17
	Flour	0.19
	Beef	0.70
	Pork	0.80
	Tomatoes (summer)	0.01
	Vegetables	0.02
	Oil	0.88
	Chicken, duck	0.70
Bicycle		140.00
Sewing machine		140.00
Camera		70.00
Fashionable shoes		10.00
Bus pass per month		3.50

Twelve hours on the plane. The group of Alsatians noisily celebrate the fiftieth birthday of one of their number: songs, applause, present, champagne. At first irritating, then disarming.

Draw clear distinction between Pi-Lin Pi-Kong campaign and the Beethoven–Antonioni incidents. Campaign: yes, serious, fundamental. Beethoven? probably now perceived as a mistake. Antonioni? minor, to be extinguished (unleashed mainly because of the links between Antonioni and the PCI): this was said yesterday by the Luxingshe Boss, really cross at having lost two hundred passengers from a Cruise of the liner *France* at Guangzhou, thanks to the Tourists' fear of the 'Barbarity' of the Chinese.

Those Alsatians, back there, are kicking up a racket! (Like any French group: full of self-assurance.) While in front, six charming, quiet negroes . . .

The Air France lunch is so vile (bread rolls like pears, shapeless chicken in greasy sauce, coloured salad, cabbage with chocolaty starch, and more Champagne!) that I'm on the verge of writing a letter of complaint. Chicken basquaise over the Himalayas! Window dressing yet again.

Stop-off at Karachi. Very hot: Nothing to buy (how awful). But the whole western world comes back to me: the tricks and eroticism of three charming Pakistanis. I'd like to come back here!

So it would be necessary to pay for the Revolution with everything I love: 'free' discourse exempt from all repetition, and immorality.

Reading through my notes to make an index, I realize that if I were to publish them as they are, it would be exactly a piece of Antonioni. But what else can I do? In fact, one has just the choice between:
– approving. Discourse 'in': impossible
– criticizing. Discourse out: impossible
– describing a stay in no particular order. Phenomenology. Antonioni. 'Criminal'! 'Perfidious intention and despicable method'.[38]

Chinese: basically: Quakers (they conquer Marxist America) (the women are nuns).

A big beanpole (from the group of Alsatians) keeps walking up and down the central aisle: as if he were overseeing galley slaves.

Begin the text (if I write one) with: the two plane meals: Air France, vile; describe ≠ Chinese: two apples, tea, towel, cigarettes.
This evening: two slices of beetroot, some cucumber, tomato = salad + sauce in plastic sachet (salmon) + burning but not hot fat from meat + peas + dry, heavy cake: old, tasteless pastry plastered over it.]

Summary: three admirations, two resistances, one question.
I   1. Satisfaction of needs
       2. Intermixing of layers
       3. Style, Ethics
II   1. Stereotypes
       2. Morality
III   Place of Power

— Notes —

1 The *Quotidien de Paris* had just been founded by Philippe Tesson, in April 1974. It closed in 1996. Barthes is alluding to *Retour à l'URSS* (1936; English tr. *Return from the USSR* by Dorothy Bussy, 1937) and *Retouches à mon retour de l'URSS* (1937; English tr. by Bussy, *Afterthoughts on the USSR*, 1938), in which André Gide criticizes Stalinism. (*The numbered notes are by Anne Herschberg Pierrot.*)

2 *La Poudre aux yeux* [literally 'powder in the eyes', figuratively 'window dressing' – Tr.] is a two-act comedy by Eugène Labiche (1861).

3 These initials may be a reference to Claude Lévi-Strauss, who devotes a chapter to the analyses of Marcel Granet in *Structures élémentaires de la parenté* (1949; English tr. by J. H. Bell, J. R. von Sturmer, and R. Needham, *Elementary Structures of Kinship*, 1969).

4 Jean Yanne's film *Les Chinois à Paris* (1974) presents a stereotyped picture of China.

5 'Supports-Surfaces' is the name of a group of contemporary French artists (Vincent Bioulès, Daniel Dezeuze, Claude Viallat, and others) which came together at the end of the 1960s. They sought to rethink the basic components of painting.

6 Barthes's mistake for Saturday, 13 April.

7 The commune of Sino-Romanian Friendship was located next to the Marco Polo Bridge (Lugou Qiao) near Beijing. This tenth-century bridge, described in admiring terms by Marco Polo, has retained its celebrity thanks to the incident of 7 July 1937 which marked the outbreak of the Sino-Japanese War.

8 The revolutionary committees were set up between January 1967 and autumn 1968, during the Cultural Revolution, and symbolized the seizure of power from the former cadres. Initially comprising the 'triple alliance' of rehabilitated cadres, representatives of the masses, and representatives of the army, they came under army control in 1968 and played an important role in restoring order.

9 Mutual aid groups marked the first stage of collectivization. They brought together several households, often linked by family ties. The second stage was the cooperatives, of a lesser type (20 to 50 families, semi-socialist) or a higher type (120 to 250 families, socialist): these

became widespread in the middle of the 1950s. The policy of the 'Great Leap Forward' led to the introduction of people's communes, as developed in summer 1958. They were built up on the basis of a production team, with a production brigade above them; this latter corresponded to the former superior cooperatives, and also managed certain public amenities. The rural people's commune was simultaneously a collectivized unit of agricultural production which could include 5,000 families and more, and a unit of industrial production. It also performed a social, educative, administrative, and political function, under the authority of the party committee, as well as a military role. Subsequently, the people's communes were reduced and made more flexible, becoming purely administrative entities. They came to an end in 1984, with decollectivization.

10 This is Li Sian, the vice-president of the Commune.

11 Yuan: Chinese currency. 1 yuan = 100 fen.

12 Inspired by the example of the Canadian doctor Norman Bethune (1890–1939), who had placed himself at the service of the Red Army, Mao Zedong launched the idea of 'barefoot doctors' in 1965. These were medical workers who practised in the country after following a short period of medical training (three to six months). The system was complemented, from 1966 onwards, by young town-dwelling medical students sent to the countryside. The policy of barefoot doctors was abandoned in the 1980s.

13 'The Liberation' refers to the Communists' victory over the Kuomintang in 1949. The People's Republic of China was founded on 1 October.

14 The delegation of *Tel Quel* and its companions arrived in China at the height of the campaign against Confucius and Lin Biao, the so-called 'Pi-Lin Pi-Kong campaign'. This campaign was unleashed at the end of the 10th Congress of the Chinese Communist Party in August 1973 by the left wing of the Cultural Revolution, and was directed firstly against Confucius and, through him, against Zhou Enlai and the moderate elements then starting to return to power, such as Deng Xiaoping. The radicals endeavoured to link this critique to the need to raise the profile of the Cultural Revolution. From February 1974 onwards, the campaign was also aimed at Lin Biao, who was associated with Confucius, and it implemented various efforts to stir up the masses. The campaign was gradually taken over by the moderates, who modified its themes, especially emphasizing the merits of production. It faded away at the end of the year.

15 'New China', National Printing Works of Beijing (see Marcelin Pleynet, *Journal de voyage en Chine* [Paris: Hachette, 1980], p. 14).

16 Marshal Lin Biao, one of the Red Army's most brilliant generals, played a major role in unleashing the Cultural Revolution, enabling Mao to rely on army support against the Party leadership. Mao Zedong's 'closest comrade-in-arms', designated as his successor in 1969, subsequently vanished in circumstances that have yet to be made clear. He was alleged to have plotted against Mao's life. According to the official version, he fled with his family by plane to the Soviet Union and was killed in the Trident, which crashed in Mongolia in September 1971.

17 These are always: Marx, Engels, Lenin, Stalin.

18 In 1974, Enver Hoxha's Albania was part of the Maoist China camp, and could draw on its technical, financial, and military aid.

19 After the failure of the Great Leap Forward and the subsequent famine, Liu Xiaoqi and other officials adopted a pragmatic and quite liberal economic policy. Liu was the main target and one of the first victims of the Cultural Revolution: expelled from the Party in 1967, then forced out of office as President of the Republic, he died in detention in 1969. He was later rehabilitated in 1980. The Great Proletarian Cultural Revolution was unleashed by Mao, and took the form of a struggle for power, with the Party apparatus as its target. As a movement, it was based on the violent insurrection of the Red Guards (1966–7), with order being re-established under the aegis of the army in 1968–9. It ended, in the official version of events, with the death of Mao in 1976.

20 A 'brick' is a stereotypical, phraseological unit. 'In fact, every discourse seems to progress by means of commonplaces ("topoi" and clichés), analogous to the sub-programs known in cybernetics as "bricks"' (Barthes, 'Alors, la Chine?', *OC* IV, p. 518). [The word *'brique'* means something like 'module' in computer language, but as Barthes seems to draw on its more basic meaning as 'brick', a heavy, mass-produced block out of which to construct a discourse, I have translated it as such – Tr.]

21 In the *Critique of the Gotha Programme* (1875, published by Engels in 1891), Karl Marx criticizes the draft programme of the Social Democrats, which the two organizations of the German working class wished to submit to the unification congress that met at Gotha in May 1875. This text was one of the main reference points in the campaign against Confucius and Lin Biao.

22 For *dazibao*, see next note (23). In the *Critique of the Gotha Programme*, Karl Marx attacks the ideas of Lassalle, the founder of the General German Workers' Association, and the inspiration – via the 'Lassalleans' – behind the idealistic programme of the Social Democrats of Gotha.

23 *Dazibao* are posters or notices written in large, handwritten calligraphic characters, with a political content. Barthes transcribes the word as *Ta*

Tsi Pao, an unusual transcription, but Maria Antonietta Macchiocchi, in her *Daily Life in Revolutionary China* (first published in Italian, 1971; English tr. 1972) also transcribes it as *tatʒupao*.

24 There is an echo of this question in 'And if I hadn't read . . .', a fragment of *Roland Barthes by Roland Barthes* (first published in French, 1975; English tr. by Richard Howard [London: Macmillan, 1977]), which Barthes was then writing.

25 The attitude of Zhao the guide can probably be explained by his suspect past. Barthes writes the name of the guide as 'Chao', but it is here transcribed the way it appears in Marcelin Pleynet's *Le Journal du voyage en Chine*, in pinyin, the standard transcription.

26 See previous note.

27 The Peace Hotel, on the Bund in Shanghai, along the River Huangpu, in the former international concessions, was opened in 1929, and it is now preserved as a landmark of 1930s architecture, together with the other buildings of the Bund.

28 Key notion of Chinese philosophy, especially Daoism. The '*dao*' is the fundamental force flowing through all things; by metonymy, in the martial arts, it refers to a succession of movements – a way leading to the mastery of the art, and to unity.

29 I.e. the refurbishing of the hull of a ship.

30 The accusation of revisionism (in the sense of an 'ideological position advocating the revision of a dogmatically fixed political doctrine', as the French *Petit Robert* dictionary defines it) is used in the context of China to describe deviations from the Maoist line, in this case the economic policy of Liu Xiaoqi at the start of the 1960s, presented as 'revisionist'. The term is also associated with the post-Stalinist policies of the USSR ('Soviet revisionism'). On Liu Xiaoqi, see also note 19, p. 199.

31 See p. 25.

32 Lin Biao had been one of the guiding lights of the Cultural Revolution. The 'Pi-Lin' campaign identified this leftist standpoint with an attitude that was actually right-wing and counter-revolutionary. The quotation may refer to a speech made by Mao Zedong in 1945, quoted in the *Little Red Book* (ch. XVII): 'We should be modest and prudent, guard against arrogance and rashness, and serve the Chinese people heart and soul.'

33 The Nanjing Bridge over the Yangzi is a landmark Chinese achievement. Of strategic importance, it is a recurrent point of reference, and an obligatory stop-off point for travellers. Completed in 1968, during the Cultural Revolution, it is more than 6 kilometres long and comprises two levels, one for trains and one for cars.

34 Shanghai was attacked on 13 August 1937 by the Japanese Army, and fell on 7 November after a siege lasting almost three months.

35 *Di yin*, in traditional Chinese literature, designates a 'sentimental song', usually a rhythmic poem.

36 Antonioni had managed to produce a documentary on China (*Chung Kuo, Cina (China)*, 1972) that provoked harsh criticism, mainly from Mao's wife Jiang Qing and her circle. The attacks on Antonioni, in late January 1974, were part of the campaign against Confucius and Lin Biao and in fact were aimed at destabilizing Zhou Enlai, who had invited Antonioni to direct his film.

37 The *lectio*, a scholastic method of education in the Middle Ages, was the reading of, and commentary on, a canonical text, ensuring that it was fully understood.

38 Abbreviated word: reading conjectural.

39 The Kuomintang (or Guomindang), the 'National People's Party', was founded by Sun Yat-Sen in 1911, and in 1923 formed a united front with the Chinese CP, which obtained important posts in the nationalist party. On the death of Sun Yat-Sen (1925), Chiang Kai-shek took over the movement. He broke the union in 1927, with the '12 April coup' (disarmament and massacre of union and Communist militants in Shanghai, followed by an anti-Communist purge in the regions he controlled). On 1 August, the civil war began.

40 This might be Grigori Voitinsky (1893–1953), secretary of the 'Far East Bureau' of the Comintern, who seems to have played a part in organizing the 1st Congress of the CCP.

41 Chen Duxiu, Party Secretary from 1921 to 1927, was deprived of his post at the meeting of 7 August 1927, by the Central Committee of the CCP, under Stalin's influence. He was accused of 'rightist capitulationism' after the setbacks suffered by the Communists between April and January. Chen Duxiu was criticized for his lukewarm stance towards the alliance with the Kuomintang, and was excluded from the Party in 1929, after which he became a leader of the Trotskyist movement.

42 This famous aphorism of Mao Zedong comes from a 1938 text ('Problems of War and Strategy'), reprinted in *The Little Red Book* ch. 5, 'War and Peace'.

43 Qu Qiubai replaced Chen Duxiu in August 1927 and was himself ousted from the leadership of the Party ('first opportunistic leftist deviation') in 1928. Li Lisan took over instead, becoming *de facto* general secretary. Accused of the second leftist deviation of the Party, Li Lisan, the supporter of an urban revolution based on the trade unions, was held responsible for the Communist military defeats of 1930 and ousted, with power

passing to the delegate of the Kuomintang and his team, including Wang Ming. The latter was subsequently accused of the 'third leftist deviation'.

44 Zhang Guotao, who led the IV Army, had opposed Mao on the strategy of the Long March in summer 1935.

45 In February 1954 Gao Gang was accused of dissidence, officially on the charge that he had tried to create an autonomous base (an 'independent kingdom') in the provinces of the North-East. Gao Gang committed suicide in 1954, and his purging was made public only a year later. The Party went through another significant crisis in August 1959 with the ousting of Marshal Peng Dehuai, for his opposition to the policy of the Great Leap Forward and the people's communes.

46 The 3rd International (the Comintern) was created in Moscow in 1919 and was dominated by Stalin from 1924. It imposed on the CCP collaboration with the Kuomintang, which lasted until 1927, the year when the Chinese workers' movement was crushed. For Lucien Bianco (*The Origins of the Chinese Revolution, 1915–1949*, tr. by Muriel Bell, new edn [Stanford, Calif.; London: Stanford University Press, Oxford University Press, 1973]), the two main mistakes made by the CCP under the influence of Moscow were to underestimate the danger represented by Chiang Kai-shek and to wager on the working-class uprisings rather than to play the peasant card.

47 All these accusations came from Stalinist propaganda against Trotsky (this was particularly violent during the Moscow trials of 1936–7): sabotage, espionage, collusion with Japan, and Hitler's Germany.

48 Luxun (1881–1936) is considered to be the founder of modern Chinese literature, written in a vernacular style, especially in the novella (*Diary of a Madman*, 1918), and in 1918 he was one of the creators of the League of Left-Wing Writers.

49 The Palais Galliera in Paris held exhibitions on fashion and objets d'art before becoming, in 1977, the Museum of Costume and Fashion.

50 Always Marx, Engels, Lenin, and Stalin.

51 The Volga came out in 1956; it was the main car of the Soviet era.

52 'Grass' refers to the cursive style of Chinese calligraphy.

53 On Mao's initiative, the Great Leap Forward (1958–61) aimed at accelerating the building of socialism, in rivalry with the Soviet Union, through a new voluntarist economic programme: the mobilization of the masses, a programme of major public works, an increase in collectivization with the creation of huge people's communes. It was a failure, and led to a terrible famine.

54 The Luxingshe Agency (sometimes just 'The Agency') is the official Chinese agency for tourism, translation, and political communication.

55 *La Nouvelle critique: Revue de marxisme militant* (1948–80), the review that was attacked by *Tel Quel*, was the official review of the French Communist Party. *La Pensée: Revue du rationalisme moderne* was close to the French CP.

56 A probable allusion to the epistemological break defined by Louis Althusser as occurring between the texts of the young Marx before 1845 and the texts of historical materialism. (See the Preface to Althusser, *For Marx*, tr. by Ben Brewster [London: Verso, 2010]). Louis Althusser taught at the École normale supérieure in the rue d'Ulm, Paris, from 1948 to 1980.

57 Barthes is here referring to the violent quarrel between Francis Ponge and Marcelin Pleynet, which marked Ponge's break with *Tel Quel*. Francis Ponge had criticized an article by Marcelin Pleynet on Braque published in *Art Press*, in a tract with the title: 'Mais pour qui donc se prennent maintenant ces gens-là?' ('But who the hell do those people now think they are?') Marcelin Pleynet published a reply 'Sur la morale politique' ('On political morality'), dated March, in the summer 1974 issue of *Tel Quel*.

58 This is a reference to the Éditions du Seuil.

59 Karl Marx, *Critique of the Gotha Programme*; Lenin, *Imperialism, the Highest Stage of Capitalism* (1916, published in 1917); Mao Zedong, 'On the Correct Handling of Contradictions within the People' (a speech of 27 February 1957). Engels first published the *Theses on Feuerbach* (written by Marx in 1845) as an appendix to Friedrich Engels, *Ludwig Feuerbach and the End of Classical German Philosophy* (1888), in a modified version.

60 The official press broadcast the 'bricks' of the campaign against Confucius and Lin Biao. Lin Biao's defence of 'genius' was linked to the thought of Confucius (themes such as the 'will of heaven' and 'innate knowledge', or philosophers who are 'born wise' . . .). See the collection of articles published by Claude Schmitt, *Critique de Lin Biao et de Confucius (pi-lin pi-kong), janvier–décembre 1974* (Geneva: Alfred Eibel éditeur, 1975).

61 Lin Biao opposed Mao on essential points; in particular, he criticized the policy of rapprochement with the United States. The story of the Lin Biao affair is based on rumours. In spring 1971, worried by his own isolation, Lin Biao allegedly envisaged a *coup d'état* with the help of a group of partisans and his son Lin Liguo, with the details of the plot appearing in the document '5-7-1' (*wuqiyi*, an expression that, when pronounced with different tones, can mean 'armed insurrection'). When the plan fell through in September, Lin Biao is said to have fled, dying in a plane crash in Mongolia. (See also note 16, p. 199.)

62 The Confucianist School emphasized law that was based on morality, respect for the hierarchy and the rites, in a patriarchal society, whereas the Legalists advocated a government based on written rules. 221 BC was the start of the reign of the mythical founder of China, the Legalist emperor, Qin Shi Huang Di.

63 On the '571 plan', see p. 49 and note 61, p. 203.

64 Wang Chong (AD 27–100) criticized Confucius in a chapter of his 'Critical Essays' (*Lungheng*). He was an author drawn on in the campaign against Confucius. The second philosopher was probably Han Feizi (who died in 233 BC), a theorist who synthesized Legalist theory (Anne Cheng, *Histoire de la pensée chinoise* [Paris: Seuil, 1997], p. 234). The two philosophers are mentioned by Julia Kristeva in the interviews in *About Chinese Women*, tr. by Anita Barrows (London: Boyars, 1977), pp. 171 and 177.

65 A reference to Lenin's critique, in the name of materialism, of the neo-Kantian idealist positions of the 'Machianists', the disciples – especially the Russian disciples – of the philosopher and physicist Ernst Mach, who, with Richard Avenarius, founded empiriocriticism (Lenin, *Materialism and Empiriocriticism*, 1908).

66 *Taking Tiger Mountain by Strategy*, a revolutionary Beijing opera, was one of the eight 'model works' authorized during the Cultural Revolution.

67 On the Nanjing Bridge, see note 33, p. 200.

68 'Count on your own strength', one of the slogans of the Great Leap Forward, repeated in the *Little Red Book*, was particularly applied to the years during which Soviet aid was stopped. In July 1960, Moscow recalled its experts, and suspended its cooperation with China.

69 The Académie de la Grande Chaumière, founded in 1902, at 14, rue de la Grande Chaumière, in Montparnasse, was a prestigious school of art in Paris at the start of the twentieth century.

70 Barthes is here referring to the Centre expérimental de Vincennes, created in 1969, now the University of Paris-8.

71 (Barthes's spelling.) This instrument with plucked strings, a sort of Chinese lute or mandolin, is actually a 'pipa'.

72 This is the producer Fernand Lombroso, who presented the Beijing Circus in Paris in France from the 1960s onwards. Barthes saw the show in Paris.

73 *The Dream of the Red Chamber* by Cao Xueqin (1723–63) is a classic of Chinese literature, interpreted during the campaign against Confucius as an anti-Confucian political novel. See the article by Ren Du (April 1974), translated into French in *Tel Quel*, 60, winter 1974.

Notebook 2

1 'In the train a quarrel between Ph. S. and our guide Zhao who asks Ph.
  S. to check the translation of the slogans of the current campaign against
  Confucius and Lin Biao. Ph. S. does so and tells Zhao that he'd like
  to copy this list. Zhao refuses' (Marcelin Pleynet, *Journal de voyage en
  Chine*, p. 50).

2 Barthes linked these three notions closely together from his work
  Empire of Signs onwards (published in French as *L'Empire des Signes*
  [Geneva: Albert Skira, 1970]; English tr. by Richard Howard [London:
  Cape, 1972]). The incident of the haiku is 'what falls, what makes a
  fold and yet isn't anything else' (Barthes, *La préparation du roman*, ed.
  by Natalie Léger [Paris: Seuil-IMEC, 2003], p. 94), or, unlike the accident, it is 'simply *what falls* gently, like a leaf, on life's carpet; it is that
  faint, fugitive crease given to the fabric of days; it is what can be *just
  barely* noted' (Barthes, 'Pierre Loti, "Aziyadé"', *New Critical Essays*, tr.
  by Richard Howard [New York: Hill and Wang, 1980], p. 108). In *Le
  Monde*, 24 May 1974, Barthes would refer to the 'drabness' (*fadeur*) of
  China.

3 See Notebook 1.

4 Michel Jobert, the French Minister for Foreign Affairs (1973–4),
  denounced the 'American–Soviet condominium' over the world, and
  opposed United States interference in European affairs.

5 The mausoleum of the founder of the first Republic of China, proclaimed
  in Nanjing in 1912.

6 On the criticism made of Antonioni, see Notebook 1, p. 29 and note 36,
  p. 201.

7 Tomb of Zhu Yuanzhang (1328–98), first emperor of the Ming dynasty
  (fourteenth–seventeenth century). His successors transferred their
  capital to Beijing and were buried in the 'valley of the thirteen tombs' to
  the north of Beijing.

8 The directive of 7 May 1966 encouraged the creation of the campaign
  for schools – later known as the '7 May Campaign' – in which cadres,
  students, and intellectuals from the towns were to perform manual
  labour and undergo ideological re-education. These schools were set
  up in former Party schools, in state farms, or in former labour camps.
  Discipline in them was very harsh.

9 The Red Guards were mainly composed of students and high-school
  students. They became the emblem of the Cultural Revolution, which
  relied on their insurrection. In 1966, they rose in violent rebellion against
  cadres who were stubbornly 'refractory' to Maoist thought; in autumn

1967, they were demilitarized, then sidelined a year later and sent in huge numbers to the countryside, for re-education.

10 Reading conjectural.

11 *The People's Daily* is the official newspaper of the People's Republic of China.

12 'To go against the tide' was the new political slogan of summer 1973, accompanying the nascent campaign against Confucius and then Lin Biao. Simon Leys reports similar details: the revolt of a student against an exam system that treated with contempt the achievements of the Cultural Revolution (*Broken Images: Essays on Chinese Culture and Politics*, tr. by Steve Cox [London: Allison and Busby, 1979].

13 The Algerian President Houari Boumediene had gone to China in February 1974.

14 In the 1960s, and again around 1970, the brigade of Dazhai in Shanxi, North China, was held up as an example in the struggle against peasant individualism. Chen Yonggui, Party Secretary of this unit, was a famous personality. The brigade was a model of renunciation of the private patch of ground, of the dividing out of work-points in accordance with political attitude, and self-sufficiency ('counting on your own strength'), and it supposedly undertook major work on irrigation and soil improvement without drawing on state aid. Later disclosures brought out the mythical character of the experience of Dazhai, whose inhabitants in fact used state resources and army help.

15 After the famine of the years 1959–61, in February 1962, Liu Xiaoqi ensured that the *sanziyibao* ('three freedoms and one guarantee') were adopted, as the initial stage in de-collectivization: the distribution of collective lands between peasant homesteads, which then committed to providing the state with part of their production at a low cost, and were free to do what they wanted with the rest. This was actually close to the NEP (New Economic Policy), an economic liberalization implemented in Russia by Lenin in 1921, as a result of the situation ensuing from the First World War and the Civil War.

16 Lin Biao was accused of organizing the cult of Mao in an attempt to separate him from the masses.

17 Founded AD c. 68, this monastery was the first Buddhist temple in China. Burned down during the Cultural Revolution, it did not reopen until the 1980s.

18 The peony was the emblem of Luoyang, which was the capital of several dynasties in ancient China.

19 HBMs (*Habitations à Bon Marché* – inexpensive dwellings) were a form of social housing, prefiguring the HLMs (*Habitations à Loyer Modéré* –

low-rent housing, i.e. council flats). The HBMs were developed in the 1920s and 1930s, mainly in Paris and its suburbs.

20 One of the main sites of Buddhist rock carving in China, begun in the late fifth century under the Dynasty of the Northern Wei (386–534) and continued for about four hundred years until the dynasty of the Northern Song (960–1127). Most of the works date from the Northern Wei and the Tang dynasty (618–907).

21 The expression 'American imperialism' (with the obligatory epithet, as in the tradition of Homeric epithets) occurs in Barthes's rhetorical analysis of Maoist phraseology.

22 See note 2, p. 205 and Simon Leys, who writes: 'In the tours for foreign visitors, always superbly organized, anything that might be unpredictable, unexpected, spontaneous, or improvised is ruthlessly eliminated. Leisure, too: the visitors' programmes are arranged to keep them on the go from dawn to late at night' (*Chinese Shadows*, no translator [Harmondsworth: Penguin, 1978], p. 2).

23 The question mark replaces '40%', which has been crossed out.

24 Nikita Khrushchev became First Secretary of the Party in 1953, after the death of Stalin. He launched de-Stalinization in February 1956, at the 20th Congress of the Communist Party of the Soviet Union, in which he denounced Stalin and the cult of personality. The Chinese were reluctant to de-Stalinize and were in increasing disagreement with USSR policies – Chinese nationalism conflicted with the Soviet desire to lead the Socialist camp. The Chinese leadership seems to have viewed Khrushchev's personal role as a determining factor in these dissensions. There was a final breakdown in relationships in July 1960 with the sudden withdrawal of Soviet experts and the suspension of current agreements on scientific and technical agreement so as to bring pressure to bear on Chinese policies.

25 The details are given later, p. 108.

26 Barthes comments on this idea in regard to the films of Eisenstein: '[T]he Eisensteinian "people" is essentially *lovable*' ('The Third Meaning: research notes on several Eisenstein stills', in *The Responsibility of Forms: Critical Essays on Music, Art and Representation*, tr. by Richard Howard [Oxford: Basil Blackwell, 1985], pp. 41–62; p. 51).

27 Mencius, a Latinized form of Mengzi (Master Meng, *c.* 380 BC–289 BC), was a philosophical successor of Confucius, who was also a target in the Pi-Lin Pi-Kong campaign.

28 Marx, *Critique of the Gotha Programme* (1875, published in 1891), Lenin, *The State and Revolution* (1917), *Imperialism: The Highest Stage of Capitalism* (1916, published in 1917).

29 Alain Peyrefitte, *Quand la Chine s'éveillera . . . le monde tremblera* (Paris: Fayard, 1973).

30 'The pregnant moment' is the perfect moment of a composition. 'This perfect moment is something that Diderot, of course, had thought of (and thought through). [. . .] This crucial moment, totally concrete and totally abstract, is what Lessing later called (in *Laocoön*) the *pregnant moment*' ('Diderot, Brecht and Eisenstein', in Barthes, *The Responsibility of Forms*, pp. 89–97; p. 93).

31 An allusion to *A Woman of Thirty* by Honoré de Balzac (1824).

32 In 1964, the general political department of the army published the famous *Book of Quotations of President Mao*, known as the *Little Red Book*. Over the following years, nearly a thousand million copies were printed.

33 This could be 'Tangdu' ('capital of the Tang dynasty'), Luoyang being one of the two capitals of the Tang, together with Xi'an.

34 Qiao Yulu, a famous village official and a model hero.

35 In *The Civil War in France*, Marx commented on the insurrection of the Paris Commune (18 March–28 May 1871), which became a major revolutionary point of reference.

36 The agrarian reform of 1950 replaced the complex hierarchy of traditional village life by a new hierarchy based on social criteria that included political criteria. The Party drew on the support of the 'poor and medium-poor peasants', whom it privileged.

37 'Sitting peacefully, doing nothing, / Spring comes and the grass grows up of its own accord', a Zenzin poem from the *Zenzin Kushu* (fifteenth century) in the Zen tradition, quoted in Barthes, *Incidents*, tr. by Richard Howard (Berkeley: University of California Press, 1992), p. 38, and *Vita nova* (OC V, p. 1011).

38 Confucius (in Chinese Kong Qiu) is known as Kongfuzi ('Master Kong'), a name Latinized as Confucius by Jesuit missionaries in China in the sixteenth century.

39 Simon Leys also reports on the 'Used Razor Blade gambit, which crops up time and time again: the traveller leaves a used razor blade in his hotel room, and it is scrupulously returned to him at each stop on his trip' (*Chinese Shadows*, p. 2).

40 Xi'an station 'was built in 1933 in a traditional style, with a frescoed ceiling supported by big columns in vivid red, and elaborate woodwork in mahogany colour' (Marcelin Pleynet, *Journal de voyage en Chine*, p. 83).

41 Administrative centre of the Cantal department in south-central France, where Georges Pompidou was born, and of which he was the *député* before becoming French President (1969–74).

42 The village of Huxian, made famous during the Cultural Revolution by

the naïve paintings of its villagers, had become the model of the creative art of the people as opposed to bourgeois academic art.

43 Friedrich Engels, *Anti-Dühring* (1878).

44 See note 30, p. 208.

45 The 10th Congress of the Party, which met from 24 to 28 August 1973, ratified the posthumous exclusion of Lin Biao and demonstrated the promotion of a left-wing 'counter-current'.

46 The '*objet petit a*', very fashionable in the 1970s, designates, in the work of Lacan, the object of desire as lack.

47 The ancient source of the hot waters of Huaqingshi.

48 Since the early 1930s, Japan had occupied Manchuria and was making incursions into Chinese territory. The Communist Party called for union, but Chiang Kai-shek wanted to destroy the Red Army before fighting the Japanese, which provoked nationalist reactions among the Chinese. He was arrested at Xi'an on 12 December 1936 by one of his generals, the young 'warlord' Zhang Xueliang, who had retreated with his troops from Manchuria. However, under pressure from the Comintern, negotiations led to the freeing of Chiang Kai-shek and the suspension of hostilities against the Communists. The 'Xi'an incident' led, a few months later, to a united front of the Communist Party and the Kuomintang against the Japanese enemy.

49 In other words, with reference to the etymology, a 'founder of language': Sade, Fourier, Loyola, are 'Logothetes, founders of language' (Barthes, *Sade/Fourier/Loyola*, tr. by Richard Miller [London: Cape, 1977], p. 3). 'Nomothetes', on the other hand, are 'founders of laws' (in Greek antiquity, the term designated the members of a legislative assembly).

50 *The White-Haired Girl* was a famous Chinese revolutionary ballet. It showed the history of a young girl forced to flee into a mountain cave after her father was beaten to death for refusing to marry her off to an old landlord. In *Jocelyn*, a poem 8,000 lines long, which was to be the last episode of a huge humanitarian epic (1836), Lamartine celebrates the grandeur of sacrifice. While at a seminary, Jocelyn flees the Terror and takes refuge in a cave in the Dauphiné. Here he shelters the son of a mortally wounded outlaw, in reality a girl with whom he falls in love. But he has to renounce his chaste passion in order to be a priest.

Notebook 3

1 The place where Barthes had a country house, near Bayonne.

2 This is Jean-Paul Laurens (1838–1921), a painter of historical scenes.

3 The destination of the Long March in 1935, Yan'an became the Communist capital, in the main base set up by the Communists in North-Shaanxi. It was the point of departure for the conquest of power. Within the framework of the agreement between the Communist Party and the Kuomintang for a 'united front' against the Japanese aggressor, in 1937 the Red Army became the 8th Road Army.

4 Zhou Enlai played an active role in negotiations with the Kuomintang at the time of the 'Xi'an incident' and during the period leading up to the agreement between the two parties. The 'united front' between Communists and Nationalists was not, however, without major tensions. Chiang Kai-shek established a blockade of the Yan'an base and other Communist bases until the Japanese attack of May 1941.

5 The sentence is incomplete.

6 Reading conjectural.

7 Open civil war began officially in 1946, but it was preceded by several armed incidents.

8 Eisenstein's film depicts the mutiny of sailors on board the Battleship Potemkin in June 1905 at Odessa, in Tsarist Russia.

9 'Autonymy' describes the use of a word (an utterance) that designates itself as a sign in discourse ('"Cat" has three letters'). Barthes applies this reflexivity to photography.

10 Alcoholic drink with a sorghum base.

11 See Notebook 2, p. 131.

12 Barthes several times quotes Baudelaire's words about Delacroix, 'the grandiloquent truth of gestures on life's great occasions' (in Baudelaire's *Curiosités esthétiques*). It is the epigraph of 'The world of wrestling' (Barthes, *Mythologies*, tr. by Annette Lavers [London: Cape, 1972], pp. 15–25; p. 38) and is also found in *Roland Barthes by Roland Barthes* (in the section called 'The numen', p. 134).

13 Does 'I' mean 'Ideology', or 'Imaginary'?

14 Dinglin ('Tomb of Tranquillity'), by Wanli (1573–1620), thirteenth emperor of the Ming dynasty (1402–24).

15 Changling, tomb of the Yongle ('Eternal Joy'), the third emperor of the Ming dynasty.

16 Barthes is probably referring to those little enamelled structures in yellow, like kiosks, that are found around temples and monuments and in which offerings of paper, silk, etc., are burnt. Were books burnt there?

17 Probably the anthropologist and historian Lin Yaohua.

18 The Han are the majority ethnic group in China. Chinese is the 'Han language'. Ethic groups speaking a 'non-Chinese' language are considered as minorities.

19 The rising of Tibet against the Chinese military presence, in spring 1959, provoked a bloody crackdown. The Dalai Lama had to take refuge in India.
20 The expression is a conjectural reading.
21 This is Liu Xiaoqi.
22 The attacks on Beethoven and classical music were one of the themes of the campaign against Confucius and Lin Biao between January and May 1974.
23 This is Tchaikovsky's *Swan Lake*.
24 Piano score by Tekla Bądarzewska-Baranowska, also known as 'A Maiden's Prayer'.
25 *Teleute/askesis* (Greek): the final end or result / the exercise, practice, way of life.
26 This remark is found in a sort of ironic column written by Barthes during the trip to China and referring to the made-to-measure suit he wanted and was finally able to order. See p. 176.
27 The 'Polovtsian Dances' are part of the opera *Prince Igor* by Alexander Borodin (1890).
28 The martial arts.
29 The death of President Georges Pompidou on 2 April 1974 made it necessary to hold early elections, which took place shortly after the return of Barthes and the *Tel Quel* group from their trip to China, on 5 May and 19 May 1974. Valéry Giscard d'Estaing was elected with a small majority at the second round, against the candidate of the Union of the Left, François Mitterrand.
30 The SFIO (Section Française de l'Internationale Ouvrière – French Section of the Working-Class International) became the Socialist Party in 1969.
31 Reading conjectural.
32 The word at the foot of the page is missing.
33 The 9th Congress of the Chinese Communist Party, mainly composed of delegates from the Army, met in Beijing between 1 and 24 April 1969. It gave itself new statutes and broke with the 8th Congress of 1956, electing an almost completely new Central Committee. This Congress marked the victory of the Cultural Revolution, celebrated by Lin Biao, and officialized a political line based on the ideological mobilization of society.
34 See p. 177.
35 Edgar Snow, the American journalist, was one of the first to interview Mao. *Red Star Over China* (London: Victor Gollancz, 1937) told the story of the Chinese Communist Party until the 1930s, turning it into a legend.

36 Gaëtan Picon devoted a few lines to Barthes in the *Panorama de la littéra-ture française*, new revised edition (Paris: Gallimard, 1960, pp. 290–1), referring to *Michelet* by 'Roland Barthes (the author of the flavoursome, profound, and questionable *Mythologies*)', p. 290.

37 Oral abbreviation for 'revisionist'.

38 In the text 'Dear Antonioni . . .', written for the awarding of the 'Archiginnedio d'Oro' prize to Antonioni on 28 January 1980, Barthes wrote: 'It was your film on China that made we want to go there; and if this film was provisionally rejected by those who should have under-stood that the strength of its love was superior to any propaganda, this is because it was judged in accordance with a reflex of power and not in accordance with a demand for truth. The artist is without power, but he has some relationship with truth' (Barthes, *Oeuvres complètes*, V, pp. 902–3).

NOTEBOOK 4

— Notebook 4 —

CHINA

Notebooks

— [Thematic index] —

— Index of proper names —